Hippies
and
American
Values

REFERENCE

Timothy Miller

The
Hippies
and
American
Values

SECOND EDITION

The University of Tennessee Press / Knoxville

Copyright © 1991, 2011 by The University of Tennessee Press / Knoxville.
All Rights Reserved. Manufactured in the United States of America.

First edition hardcover: 1st printing, 1991.
First edition paperback: 1st printing, 1991; 2nd printing, 1992; 3rd printing, 2000;
4th printing, 2003.
Second edition paperback: 1st printing, 2011.

The paper in this book meets the requirements of American National Standards
Institute / National Information Standards Organization specification Z39.48-1992
(Permanence of Paper). It contains 30 percent post-consumer waste and is certified
by the Forest Stewardship Council.

Library of Congress Cataloging-in-Publication Data

Miller, Timothy, 1944–
The hippies and American values / Timothy Miller
        p.   cm.
Includes bibliographical references and index.

ISBN 10: 1-57233-817-2
ISBN 13: 978-1-57233-817-3

1. Hippies—United States—History.
2. Subculture—History.
3. United States—Social conditions—1960–80.
I. Title.
HQ799.7.M55   1991
305.5'68—dc20   90-48062

For Abraham
A Free Spirit

Contents

Illustrations

Acknowledgments

Many persons helped bring this study to fruition. Those who deserve the most thanks are Norman Yetman, Stephen Fox, Robert Shelton, and Pam Detrixhe, all of whom read and commented on early versions of the manuscript; my sister, Gretchen, and her family; and my wife, Tamara, and our children, Jesse and Abraham. Roger Martin provided insights at crucial junctures, as usual. Charley Shively and Janet Jacobs read later versions of the manuscript and made excellent suggestions that improved the book considerably. The library staff at the University of Kansas as usual provided timely, professional assistance. The graduate school at the university provided funding for illustrations. Former hippies in Lawrence and elsewhere provided many pleasant hours of reminiscing, which helped me to formulate my ideas. Eric Alstrom of Ann Arbor provided good and timely help in locating illustrations. Finally, the editors at the University of Tennessee Press are talented professionals; working with them has consistently been a great pleasure.

Introduction to the Second Edition

> I am in effect setting up moral codes and standards which include drugs, orgy music and primitive magic as worship rituals—educational tools which are supposedly contrary to our cultural mores; and I am proposing these standards to you respectable ministers, once and for all, that you endorse publically the private desire and knowledge of mankind in America, so to inspire the young.
>
> —Allen Ginsberg, *San Francisco Oracle,* January 1967

On a sunny afternoon in the fall of 1967, at the end of the Summer of Love, a band of San Francisco hippies solemnly filled a coffin with stereotyped artifacts of hippiedom and burned it, pronouncing as they did so the "death of hip." Hip actually lasted at least two or three years longer before it succumbed to political violence, nihilism, and—paradoxically—simultaneous widespread hostility toward and the crass commercialization of its ideas and values. However, although the four or five years that comprised the heyday of the counterculture passed into history several decades ago, the cultural legacy of the hippies remains surprisingly strong.

The hippies made a lasting impact on the whole American ethos. The counterculture, in its broad-spectrum challenge to the prevailing culture, argued that America needed a sweepingly new ethics appropriate to an age characterized by never-ending global power struggles, technocracy, urbanization, environmental catastrophe, and new psychedelic chemistry. The hippies saw themselves as the people of zero, the vanguard who would build a new society on the ruins of the old, corrupt one. They defined their task as bringing to the world a radical change of outlook—one which not only featured "new ideas" in some superficial sense (what mundane politician does not claim to have new ideas?), but a fundamentally new way of getting at living, at seeing the world. The hippies were probing root matters when, for example, they questioned the very rationality upon which Western culture has been built. To the counterculturists, reason had run its course; now it was time to return to the mystical and intuitional. The products of centuries of reason-dominated culture were thrown into question as well: the hippies rejected the industrial for the agrarian, the plastic for the natural, the synthetic for the organic. Finally, they challenged the formidable Western tradition of setting the individual on a pedestal; for the hippies, communal values stood over the rights and privileges of individual persons.

From such basic questioning of received truth the hippies began in a fragmentary, tentative way to outline a new ethics, born of the precepts of intuition and direct experience, that was often at odds with the values of the prevailing culture, in the midst of which the counterculture found itself, but also often reaffirmed some traditional values that had been nearly forgotten in Western society's headlong rush into modernity. Limning the outlines of that ethics is the task of this book.

From the earliest days of hip a few observers realized that undergirding the emergence of a new, alternative lifestyle were some distinctively new values and ethical propositions. Among the first to notice were J. L. Simmons and Barry Winograd, who in 1966 discerned a "hang-loose ethic" in the then-nascent counterculture. They saw the main features of that ethic as irreverence, experience, and tolerance.[1] A few years later, religious studies scholar William C. Shepherd probed the possibility of an important new ethical outlook when he observed that "if a code of ethics is said to be a necessary component of religion, the new youth culture, with its emphasis on honesty, integrity, gentleness, and personal freedom surely does have one, although it is vague and largely borrowed."[2]

As Shepherd suggested, the ethics of the hippies was never synthesized and promulgated in systematic form. Hip literature and culture, however, abounded with new ethical energy, and some of the more thoughtful hippies specifically proclaimed the existence of a grandly new ethics, systematic or no. Chester Anderson, a writer whose work bridged the beat and hip eras, for example, observed in 1968 that "it's the hippies who are developing an ethic and morality for an over-populated world; it's the hippies—ONLY the hippies—who are speaking to the youth of America."[3]

Most popular media coverage of the hippies focused on color and controversy—on Be-Ins, drugs, nudity, outlandish costumes, and the like. But amid the gawking a few of the more perceptive reporters saw deeper currents running in hippiedom. *Time,* for example, in a cover story on the hippies during the Summer of Love (1967), noted that a new ethical outlook was part of the hip presence:

> If there were a hippie code, it would include these flexible guidelines:
> —Do your own thing, wherever you have to do it and whenever you want.
> —Drop out. Leave society as you have known it. Leave it utterly.
> —Blow the mind of every straight person you can reach. Turn them on, if not to drugs, then to beauty, love, honesty, fun.[4]

And, surprisingly (*Time* was, after all, an influential organ of the hated Establishment), the anonymous writer found that the counterculturists did a respectable job of trying to live their ideals: "Indeed, it could be argued that in their independence of material possessions and their emphasis on peacefulness and honesty, hippies lead considerably more virtuous lives than the great majority of their fellow citizens."[5]

Ethical innovation and commitment, yes; systematic analysis, no. Hip ethics, as proclaimed in the late 1960s, was always a bit of a jumble. As Steven Tipton reflected in 1982, "the counterculture itself comprised a wide range of views, some of them at odds with one another."[6] This volume seeks to order, retrospectively, the fragments. I perceive my role in this exercise mainly as that of organizer and pedant, for the counterculture made its own case quite articulately. The brighter hippies were highly literate in their vitality; the ethics they promulgated, which I call the counterethics, was important because it offered an innovative appraisal of American culture and promulgated creative, if unorthodox, guidelines for conduct in a rapidly changing cultural milieu.

There will be no effort made here to reconcile the counterethics with any other system. At some points it obviously overlaps conventional Judeo-Christian ethical thinking, but to try to say that the counterculture represents mainly a dynamic restatement of the best of that ethical tradition misses the point, because many of its key precepts were at odds with society's received values. Here the counterethics is simply presented on its own terms.

What Was the Counterculture?

The counterculture was a romantic social movement of the late 1960s and early 1970s, mainly populated by teenagers and persons in their early twenties who through their flamboyant lifestyle expressed their alienation from mainstream American life. "Counterculture," written as one word or two, became the standard term for the movement (or nonmovement, as some would have it) after the appearance, in 1969, of Theodore Roszak's influential book *The Making of a Counter Culture.*[7] Until then several competing terms described the cultural revolt of the young. Other early contenders were "alternative culture" and "the underground."

Any culture, of course, can spawn its countercultures, and thus the hippies were part of a long tradition of cultural demurring. As Allen Ginsberg once commented, "Well, all through history, you have a bohemianism which has gone through many artistic phases and taken many forms. There's always been a continuity on the margin of people working by themselves secretly on sex, dope, art, strange ideas, or anarchism. They thought politics was shit, which every working man does also. They didn't believe in the authority of the state. They were groups of friends who hung around in interconnecting bohemian circles."[8] Their most obvious and immediate predecessors were the bohemians and beats who inhabited earlier decades of the twentieth century. The progression from beat to hip is a fairly obvious one; the beats of the 1950s advocated dropping out of society, promoted new forms of art and literature, smoked marijuana, listened to unorthodox music (jazz), rejected traditional sexual norms, and even popularized the word "hip." One of the first books (1966) to notice the first stirrings of what would become hippie culture in the East Village of New York was plausibly entitled *The New Bohemia.*[9] The connection between beat and hip was perhaps best enshrined by the name of the preeminent hip band, the Beatles. John Lennon wanted to honor the beats as well as Buddy Holly's seminal band, the Crickets.

Behind both the 1960s counterculture and its predecessor beat culture lay black America. Although the hippies were mainly white (more about that later), they were cultural outsiders, renegades who scorned the American Way of Life. Black radicals (W. E. B. DuBois, Malcolm X) were countercultural heroes because they refused to compromise with the white and prosperous Establishment. Black musicians gave heart as well as soul to hip music. (Bob Dylan and the Beatles may have been the principal hip-era cultural icons, but the energy of Chuck Berry and Little Richard wrote the grammar of rock.) Black musicians were smoking marijuana decades before white dropouts had heard of it. Norman Mailer was writing about beatniks in his 1957 essay "The White

Negro," but his observations apply equally to hippies: "It is no accident that the source of Hip is the Negro for he has been living on the margin between totalitarianism and democracy for two centuries. But the presence of Hip as a working philosophy in the sub-philosophies of American life is probably due to jazz. . . . In this wedding of the white and the black it was the Negro who brought the cultural dowry. Any Negro who wishes to live must live with danger from his first day." And, Mailer concluded, even the jargon of hip was shaped in major part by "the Negro jazzman who was the cultural mentor of a people."[10]

The counterculture's participants, usually called hippies, found themselves cast adrift from the prevailing values of society and tried, variously, to effect major changes in majority society or to drop out of it. As the hippies saw things, the Establishment—the tired, entrenched, declining prevailing system—was rotten to the core, and a new society needed to arise on its cultural dunghill. Some hippies were escapists who simply favored withdrawal from the dominant culture; others proposed much more active opposition to and confrontation with it as a necessary step on the road to cultural freedom and progress.

The counterculture had a vocal separatist minority that rejected the dominant culture wholesale and proclaimed the necessity of creating a new, independent, egalitarian society, although the means for getting there were usually murky. Separatist rhetoric could be powerful: one notable separatist document, "The Declaration of Cultural Evolution," written in 1968 by a committee including Timothy Leary, Allen Ginsberg, Paul Krassner, and Abbie Hoffman, listed, in a style imitative of the Declaration of Independence, grievances against majoritarian society—political repression, destruction of the environment, war, and the like. The declaration maintained that the counterculture had pointed the way to needed social changes, but that "many have been deaf to the voice of reason and consanguinity." Therefore, "human beings everywhere are, and quite properly ought to be, absolved from all allegiance to the present Cultural Arrangements insofar as they are obsolete and harmful."[11]

Similarly, another early theoretician of hip, Art Johnston, denounced the "Ethic of the Cool" in the West, which he defined as conformity to the status quo, the only goal of which was getting a good return on one's investment. Since, he wrote, it was very difficult to live outside the existing system, the function of the counterculture was defiance of the dominant mores. The counterculture was rebellion, a living protest vote, a declaration of choice—a Great Refusal to cooperate.[12]

Still another separatist, Jean-Jacques Lebel, wrote, in terms reminiscent of Herbert Marcuse, the radical political philosopher whose works inspired the New Left, of a "containment industry" that aimed to pacify and neutralize the American young. It operated by separating art from life (that is, by having professional artists who displaced popular spontaneous art), by advancing symbolic freedom that did not have a daily-life counterpart (as in nude theatre), and by taking a financial profit from mass-produced imitation hip culture. "This is the 'liberal' version of Hitler's 'final solution' of the youth problem. . . . I say it is time for us to create our own culture, our own lives."[13]

On the whole, however, the counterculture proposed not so much a confrontation with mainstream culture as a simple withdrawal from it. As the beat (and then countercultural) author Lawrence Lipton put it in 1968, "The hippies have passed beyond American society. They're not really living in the same society. . . . It's not so much that they're living on the leftovers, on the waste of American society, as that they just don't give a damn."[14] Or, as archetypal hippie Raymond Mungo wrote, "we . . . long ago commenced on our own total Moratorium on constructive participation in this society."[15]

Withdrawal often meant heading for a hip commune. The communes, so the theory went, were not aimed at cultural confrontation, but simply were a turning away to build a new society apart from the old. Down on the commune, a hipster wrote in 1969, "We are in Amerika, but we are no longer a part of it."[16]

From what were the hippies so alienated? Why did they see an alternative, be it confrontive or simply escapist, as necessary? The widespread sense of the counterculture was that it was simply impossible to cope with the dominant American culture any longer. America was a treadmill, a swamp of mediocrity, an emotional pressure cooker; it had become a series of meaningless institutions that transcended persons and developed lives of their own. Worse, it was all boring. Widespread mental illness and compulsive violence showed that there was a deep-running malaise in the culture; the rational alternative, as the hippies saw it, was simply to drop out.

But even dropping out was hard to do. Hippie communes were not welcome in many neighborhoods. Hip music festivals were banned at every turn. Nonviolent psychedelic chemists ended up in prison. Establishment culture, which was in the driver's seat, was not willing to tolerate the deviant behavior of the new alternative. As one hippie wrote, "They sense a threat to their continued . . . dominance. And they are absolutely correct."[17]

The Generation Gap

Age did not a hippie make or unmake (there were, after all, a few older hippies and lots of young straights), but it is abundantly clear that most counterculturists were relatively young (under thirty, as the catch-phrase had it) and that there was among the hippies great distrust of persons very far beyond adolescence. Many writers on both sides of the chasm depicted a generation gap that constituted a major battle line between youth and adults. Theodore Roszak helped promote the concept in *The Making of a Counter Culture,* depicting as critical formative agents Allen Ginsberg's 1950s poem "Howl," which condemned the parental generation by identifying it with the evil Moloch, and *Mad* magazine, which steadily presented a consistent cynicism about "adult" culture to a very large young audience.[18] Within the counterculture the generation gap was much discussed. The old was moribund; revolutionary cultural change was imminent. One polemicist, Jack G. Burgess, proclaimed,

> [You are standing on a generation that] WILL NOT BE STOOD UPON!
>
> You have declared illegal virtually every establishment, event, gathering, device, and instrument we consider important and worthwhile.
>
> [BUT] YOU CANNOT STOP THE HANDS OF TIME AND YOU CANNOT STILL THE WINDS OF CHANGE!
>
> YOU ARE DYING! Time is removing you from the face of this earth.[19]

In a more analytical frame of mind, underground writer George D. Maloney in 1968 pictured society as broadly divided into three major generations: under 30, 30–45, and over 45 in age. The problem of the 30–45 generation, he argued, was a simple one: its members were children of the Depression, were unable to shake their preoccupation with security when prosperity returned, and thus were never much concerned with human values. Maloney saw the impasse between "young" and "parental" generations as hopeless, and proclaimed, "'Tis indeed the stuff of which revolutions are made."[20]

The hopelessness of the parental generation was a common theme in the underground, but occasionally a note of a brighter future sounded. Andrew Kopkind, writing in *Rolling Stone* about the 1969 Woodstock festival, saw a phoenix of new culture rising from the ashes of "adult" American life: "What is not illusionary is the reality of a new culture of opposition. It grows out of the disintegration of the old forms, the vinyl and aerosol institutions that carry all the inane and destructive values of privatism, competition, commercialism, profitability and elitism. . . . It's not a 'youth thing' now but a generational event; chronological age is only the current phase."[21]

The Counterculture and the New Left

Although there was a widespread sense of a youth culture of opposition at least by 1967, the alternative culture was never a monolith. Broadly speaking, it embodied at least two quite different approaches to the social crisis: there was a New Left, an overtly political opposition to the dominant culture; and there was hippiedom, the world of the dropouts and cultural dissenters. Most writers analyzing the sixties have grappled with the problem of showing convergences and divergences between the "Heads" and the "Fists," as Laurence Leamer called them in his history of the early underground press.[22] Social critic Paul Goodman distinguished the two related movements in classic religious terms: the distinction involved between inward-oriented hippies and outward-oriented activists was, he said, very close to the age-old question of faith and works.[23] The majority of hippies, while often sympathetic to the New Left, weren't much interested in politics and thus saw the counterculture and New Left as distinct movements, even though the line between them was not always precise. A substantial minority, on the other hand, saw the two groups as more alike than different because they were both sworn opponents of the established regime; thus they were to be considered as fingers on one hand, distinct but sharing a common role. The visionary culture the hippies wanted to establish was based on such political ideologies as peace, racial harmony, and equality; the political crusade of the New Left was deeply romantic, and the great majority of the New Leftists lived many cultural values of the hippies, smoking marijuana, engaging in liberated sex, and often living communally.

The Australian countercultural writer Richard Neville created a typology, echoed in less precise terms elsewhere, that is useful here. Under the general heading of "The Movement," he saw three fundamental divisions: the New Left, the Underground (i.e., counterculture), and the "militant poor." The New Left consisted primarily of radical political activists, many of them members of organizations such as Students for a Democratic Society and the Student National Coordinating Committee. The militant poor consisted primarily of ethnic revolutionaries and activists, most notably African Americans, Chicanos, and Native Americans. The Underground included "hippies, beats, mystics, madmen, freaks, yippies, crazies, crackpots, communards and anyone who rejects rigid political ideology ('it's a brain disease')."[24] The New Left and the counterculture both manifested a sharp discontent with American society and its decadent hypocrisy, but they were nonetheless distinct groupings.[25]

Some hip writers minimized the differences between the two factions. As underground writer P. G. Stafford put it, "The new leftist and the acid head are in fundamental agreement at their political core. At the very least, their experience and thinking puts them both at odds with the man from the right."[26] Similarly, Stan Iverson, another underground writer, wrote, "The hippie life style has superficially influenced a broad spectrum of the United States, and is such an influence in the New Left that it is impossible—and I think un-desirable—to draw a sharp line of division between the two movements."[27] Ed Sanders, hip author and musician, observed, "We have a commonality of radicalism, smut, chromosome damage, marijuana, street fucking—we know each other."[28] Theodore Roszak also saw a basic oneness beneath the apparent differences: "We grasp the underlying unity of the countercultural variety, then, if we see beat-hip bohemianism as an effort to work out the personality structure and total life style that follow from New Left social criticism."[29] On one basic point the two schools were in harmony: something was badly wrong with American society, and each individual could do something about it.

Despite the hippies' indifference or hostility toward politics, some ob-servers argued that the counterculture actually had a more substantial politi-cal impact on American life than the New Left did, because political action among the hippies emerged from moments of real-life need and because the hippies identified the roots of modern social problems, not merely their symp-toms. Paul Goodman noted that hippies "become political when they are in-dignant . . . and they also have to work at power and politics in order to protect their business and community, e.g. against police harassment; but otherwise they rightly judge that radicals are in a bag."[30]

And whatever the normal distance between the two groups, they did work together on some important occasions. For example, at the October 1967 march on the Pentagon in protest of American involvement in Vietnam, there was a wide range of persons present.[31] Some wanted confrontation, but many merely wanted to form a human circle around the Pentagon in an attempt to levitate it! They worked together—at least for an afternoon—in rare harmony.

The counterculture faulted the New Left at several specific points. A com-mon theme was simply suspicion of organized groups in general. As Timothy Leary put it, "Mass movements make no sense to me, and I want no part of mass movements. I think this is the error that the leftist activists are making. I see them as young men with menopausal minds."[32]

Others complained that the New Left's absolutist devotion to revolution-ary activity deprived it of a humanitarian vision. "When you pick up a gun and learn to kill," wrote Mick Wheelock in the *Los Angeles Free Press,* "the part of you that loved flowers and simple things will die!"[33] "'Some people will do worse things than any cop, and do them in the name of revolution,' Eldridge Cleaver once told me," noted Raymond Mungo.[34] Ralph J. Gleason, an elder theorist of hip and a *Rolling Stone* columnist, summarized the argument: "The political radicals have the right enemies, they have courage, some of them, they even have a kind of program for Improvement of the Society which makes a kind of sense. But they all have the old approach. You can't make an omelet without breaking eggs. True, man, true. But you better figure out how to make a revolution without killing people or it won't work. We've had all that. We really have."[35] Some faulted the New Left precisely because it embraced logic and ideology; the counterculture, in varying degrees, tended to be suspicious of both. Raymond Mungo: "There are no answers! There are no systems! This is not my salvation! Leave me alone!"[36] Similarly Bob Maurice, the producer of the film *Woodstock,* contended that "contemporary radical politics is purely Christian. It's one of the manifestations of Western Christianity. And it's that dichotomy of good versus evil, essentially a Christian one, and it's idealistic. . . . [But] people are too complicated for that."[37]

Some countercultural purists protested that the New Left exploited the counterculture. "David Super-Straight" of the *Berkeley Barb,* for example, blamed the New Left for the decline of the spirit of love, for the rise of harmful drugs (as opposed to sweet dope; see chapter 1), and for the advent of guns. In particular, he accused the "Ginks of Berkeley" of having tried to organize the early hippies for their own ends, of contriving confrontations between hippies and police in the hope of politicizing the hippies, all because the Ginks wanted power for the sake of power.[38] Mungo noted that the counterculture was especially vulnerable to this sort of exploitation, and that as a result hip culture was damaged. To Mungo, political militancy was a "character disorder."[39]

Finally, the counterculture accused the New Left of losing sight of pleasure. Writing of the Woodstock festival, Greil Marcus maintained that the pleasures of dope and casual sex were and should have been undertaken because they were fun, "not because such acts represented scoring points against parents or Richard Nixon or the Reader's Digest."[40] Another observer remarked simply, "The New Left writes so many position papers that they have no time for sex. They just take a position."[41]

So the hippie counterculture and the New Left pitched their tents in distinct but adjacent campsites. The two movements could never be truly separate, if only because just behind the flash and color and irreverence of the hippies the grim reaper stood grinning: just over one's shoulder were an ugly war in Asia, a military draft, racism, and impending environmental doom.

If the hippies frequently criticized the New Left, so did the politicals criticize the culturals, and they had sufficient access to the underground press to voice their sentiments. Generally, the complaints centered on opposition to dropping out when there was so much revolutionary work to be done and to using dope and drugs, both because they sapped one's revolutionary energies and because they presented the possibility of being arrested for the wrong reason. The New Left's take on the apolitical hippies:

The psychedelic revolution is not a revolution in any sense of the word. It is a means of escaping the restlessness imposed by everyday life upon everyone in this society. But it is sterile and infantile because it does not fundamentally transform these restrictions which afflict and affect every one of us. . . .

The philosophy of the "hippies" is a philosophy of politics that says there should be love toward everyone. Love is a good thing, but hatred of what is hateful is as necessary and important.[42]

The immediate Movement reaction to drugs and dropping out was to describe it as playing into the hands of the government, allowing the creation of a totalitarian system whereby the rulers provided free drugs for the people (or at least the dissenters) in order to keep them happily and quietly oppressed. LSD was bread and circuses, the ultimate pacification program.[43]

The differences between counterculture and New Left sometimes aroused hostility on both sides. Inveterate antiwar activist David McReynolds wrote in 1967 of a meeting to plan an antiwar rally at which Richard Alpert (later known as Ram Dass) showed up and eventually delivered a long diatribe urging people to boycott the rally because some people there would burn their draft cards, and it would be "bad public relations for the psychedelic community to be involved in that kind of thing." McReynolds thereupon blasted Alpert: "I do not mock the man who seeks out the God within him. But I do mock the man who, in one breath, tells every youth to follow his own light and in the next breath warns him about public relations."[44]

Such was the typical New Leftist attitude toward the counterculture. But there was also a periodic recognition, in some leftist circles, that the hippies made an important contribution to radical politics just by their existence. No less a leftist than the radical philosopher Herbert Marcuse called the hippies "the only viable social revolution" of the day, arguing that despite their disinterest in Marxism, they were having a revolutionary impact because they opposed a repressive social system, "reject[ed] the junk they're supposed to buy now, . . . reject[ed] the war . . . reject[ed] the competitive performances."[45]

Marcuse's observations still hold up. As Andrew Kimbrell argued in 1988, the New Left's agenda was actually not a fundamental threat to society: civil rights of blacks, women, and others could be ensured by law, the war could be ended, the environment could be protected—all without making major inroads on the basic structure of society. After all, the New Left did not challenge the supremacy of reason, the notion that material prosperity is the supreme goal of society, the sanctity of economic growth, or the belief that spiritual values constituted an opiate, or at least were unimportant. By contrast, the counterculture, "though often acting in a drugged haze, attacked society at a more fundamental level than the New Left. Through experiments with lifestyles and philosophies, it challenged, if only by implication, the assumptions of most Americans about politics, knowledge, materialism, technology, and what constitutes the 'good life.'"[46]

Race, Class, and Gender in a Largely White, Male-Defined Movement

The hippies were mainly children of privilege, and their outlook reflected their heritage. They glorified poverty and sometimes lived in it; they championed the rights of racial minorities and, to some extent, women. But the movement came from a prosperous, white, male-defined segment of society. Perhaps it was inevitable that those who would reject middle-class comforts had to come from comfortable backgrounds; the have-nots of society had no excessive material luxuries to rebel against. Black hippies were unusual. They did show up occasionally, and they were readily accepted by the white majority. Their numbers, however, were never high. African Americans interested in dissent from the prevailing culture tended to be more interested in race politics than flower-child activities. It is noteworthy, though, that militant African Americans, while critical of all who would not join the revolutionary struggle, regarded the hippies as allies, not enemies. In 1968 an editorial in the *Black Panther*, the most widely read militant black publication, defined the Black Panther Party's position in its usual mince-no-words style: "Black brothers stop vamping on the hippies. They are not your enemy. Your enemy, right now, is the white racist pigs who support this corrupt system. . . . Your enemy is not the hippies. . . . WE HAVE NO QUARREL WITH THE HIPPIES. LEAVE THEM ALONE. Or the BLACK PANTHER PARTY will deal with you!"[47]

Certainly the counterculture was male defined. As the following chapters suggest, authorship in the underground press was overwhelmingly male. Women were commonly "chicks"; when they were in relationships with men, they were "old ladies." It is important to remember, however, that the heyday of the counterculture, which was in the late 1960s, came along before the prominent advent of the contemporary feminist movement, which began to attract serious, widespread attention only about 1968 or 1969, just as the counterculture was starting to wind down. At least at first, the male hippies were as disinclined as males elsewhere in society to allow women equal rights and privileges; the gap between egalitarian hippie rhetoric and male hippie actions may have had some influence on the emerging feminists, many of whom had deep roots in the counterculture. If the writers quoted in subsequent chapters tend to be male, and if hippie ideas seem largely male defined, it is because that was the dominant orientation of the hippies in their prime years.

The Counterculture and American Religion

Many ethical systems are theological or religious in basis; if the hippies had an ethics, one may naturally ask whether or not it constituted a religious movement. The answer hinges on how one defines religion. Definitions that involve institutions and rituals supporting clearly articulated religious paths would leave the hippies out; most counterculturists did not see hipness as religious per se, even if there were religious movements (such as the dope churches and various Asian-based spiritual movements) within the hip world. Definitions that involve such concepts as "ultimate concern," however, could well include the hippies. The counterculture was a movement of seekers of meaning and value, a movement that thus embodied the historic quest of any religion. Like many dissenting religionists, the hippies were enormously hostile to the religious institutions of the dominant culture, but they tried to find new and adequate ways to do the tasks the dominant religions failed to perform.

Some outside observers regarded the hippies as religious, whether the hippies liked the label or not. Harvard Divinity School professor Harvey Cox, for example, wrote, shortly after the Summer of Love (1967), that the hippies reminded him of St. Francis, that

> Hippieness represents a secular version of the historic American quest for a faith that warms the heart, a religion one can experience deeply and feel intensely. The love-ins are our 20th Century equivalent of the 19th Century Methodist camp meetings—with the same kind of fervor and the same thirst for a God who speaks through emotion and not through anagrams of doctrine. Of course, the Gospel that is preached differs somewhat in content, but then, content was never that important for the revivalist—it was the spirit that counted.
>
> Hippieness has all the marks of a new religious movement. It has its evangelists, its sacred grottoes, its exuberant converts.[48]

Similarly, religion scholar William C. Shepherd found that countercultural religiousness was patent: "Since a set of symbols, certain ritual practices, and the production of social cohesion are all marks of religious systems, it is fair to say that our counter cultural young have developed a genuine form of religiosity, indeed a quite new form for the West because it does not include doctrines or truth claims about supersensual entities."[49] Many within the counterculture itself also saw the movement as essentially a new religion, one which drew from many traditions, including Oriental and American Indian religions, as well as Western Christianity and Judaism. West Coast sexual and psychedelic activist Jefferson Poland wrote, "we find ourselves (to our surprise) in a religious revival. Simple atheism is not enough."[50] Ralph J. Gleason, the senior sage of hip, believed that religiosity could not be ignored here or anywhere: "The need to believe is there. The knowledge is implicit in life itself and the desire to believe is so overwhelming that non-belief cannot be tolerated. It is part of the life support system and it must be there."[51]

No sense of religious purpose among the hippies meant, however, that the counterculture had any fondness for the dominant religions of America. To the hippies, the churches and synagogues were mainly hoary vehicles of Establishment thought and activity in their worst form. As one hip writer summarized the critique,

> The churches are as flagrant violators of the natural, real religious way, the way of man in harmony with earth, water, sky and fire, and, of course, his fellows as any other institution. These supposed houses of worship, where one would hope, there might exist something analogous to an institutionalized conscience, are in fact just further examples of sham and hypocrisy. Rather than insist Christians as Christians in the barest sense the word conveys, refrain from supporting the golden calves our government spawns, its campaigns, its waste, its wars, the church instead functions as a Sunday salve . . . assuaging the blunted senses of each cowardly congregation . . . dressed its best for one more Sunday obligation.[52]

Self-righteous centers of hypocrisy, stations for the blessing of the Establishment, wealthy organizations mainly interested in preserving themselves, havens for the narrow-minded, anachronisms utterly irrelevant to modern life—thus were the dominant religions regarded by counterculturists. A central point of the hip rebellion was the proclamation of the New, and the prevailing religious institutions stood foursquare for the Old. They were part of the problem, not part of the solution.

There were exceptions, of course. There were radicals here and there in the mainline religions; the hippies saw the radical Catholic priests Dan and Phil Berrigan, for example, as "righteous Christians."[53] Indeed, some hippies perceived that the Establishment religions were rooted in radicalism, even though they had lost their radical perspective over history.[54] But the dissenters were not in charge in the dominant religious bodies, and radical roots were of limited value when the tree had withered.

A few saw the counterculture as a purifying element for decadent religious bodies, a revival movement that just might help restore right thinking to lost churches. As a hip couple wrote in Berkeley, "The young people we meet in the LSD underground appear to be groping toward . . . a renewal of religion, a Religion of Loving, Dancing, and Much Music. Making 'A Joyful Noise Unto the Lord!'—a personal as well as group unifying religion . . . based on 'The Unmediated Vision.'"[55]

In any event, there were divisions so profound between the hippies and the prevailing religions that expecting the hippies to have much influence on the big religions was simply unrealistic. Most hippies believed that certain drugs provided one acceptable way to try to approach the mysteries of the universe. The hippies were vocal proponents of liberated sexuality, whereas the dominant religions were society's main bastions of restricted sex. Even the most religious of the hippies tended to take unusual (by traditional American standards) approaches to religion, often emphasizing Eastern spiritual teachings, and they were often syncretistic, pursuing a sort of religiosity that combined elements ranging from Hindu mysticism to Neopaganism to Ouija boards. It's a fair guess that most hippies would not have been very welcome in most churches; for their part the hippies were usually not interested in getting active in any conventional religious body.

Resource Materials

The counterculture produced so much literature that any research, even in this digital age, must necessarily be selective in regard to its source materials. The basic body of materials that I have used has been the underground newspapers. Certainly the underground press is not the only source of data on the counterculture, nor is it necessarily the best. It was, however, the most distinctive literary creation of the counterculture and received extremely wide acceptance in the world of hip, along with attention, if not acclaim, elsewhere.[56] It also gives the researcher fairly stable materials with which to deal—much more reflective of the period than interviews conducted many years later, for example, would be. Literary materials composed by and for the counterculture may be seen in their original form by any outside observer; interviews conducted later, however much nuance and anecdote they might produce, would inevitably lean on fallible memories.

The underground press is also a valuable source in that it actually employed two media: words and visual art. The counterculture was a highly visual phenomenon, what with gaudy clothing, psychedelic posters, decorated cars and vans, and the like. The underground press was full of the distinctive and striking art of the counterculture and thus helps to convey more fully than most other materials a sense of the integration of sensory experience that the counterculture strove for. Art was understood to be one of the fronts of the multifaceted cultural revolution, and the underground press was loaded with it.

The underground papers were primary countercultural documents. They were written, edited, pasted up, and published by hippies. The underground papers were usually small, usually nonpaying, usually hand-to-mouth operations. They were papers of passion, not detachment. Thus there is no need here to try to compensate or account for the bias of the reporters; they were enthusiastic participants in the culture they were covering. Collectively, the underground papers contain, I would argue, the clearest extended statement counterculturists ever made of their ideals and values.

Thus this book uses the underground press as its primary resource because no better body of material for studying hippie culture exists. At least three substantial microfilmed collections of underground newspapers have been compiled.[57] The Bell and Howell collection, comprising sixty-eight rolls of microfilm, has excellent breadth of coverage and has provided runs of most of the papers used in this study. The collection covers 1965–1970, years that amply embrace the rise and flowering of the counterculture. (Abe Peck, in his definitive history of the underground press in both its cultural and political phases, defines his temporal turf as 1964–1973, but most of the material important to my study was published by 1970.)[58] The Bell and Howell collection contains about 500 individual periodical titles. In order to make this project manageable, I limited my research to sixty-five representative and significant titles, all from the United States. Attention was paid to selecting papers from the East and West Coasts, especially from New York City and the San Francisco Bay area, the two most important urban centers of countercultural activity, although care was also taken to sample papers from all parts of the country. Papers often cited by underground writers elsewhere as influential were included. Papers that were used were those with a generally cultural focus; those with a primarily political focus (such as some of the New Left publications, including *New Left Notes*) were omitted from the sample, as were papers with other special interests and constituencies (*Faculty Peace News, Black Panther, Free Palestine*). I read the complete run of each of the sixty-five papers as contained in the Bell and Howell collection, plus any other copies of those papers I could obtain separately.

For perspective, use has also been made of a few other miscellaneous underground papers, including some from the generally excluded categories above, and other hip writings (especially books written for the hip audience), as well as writings of sympathetic observers—Theodore Roszak and Paul Goodman are prime examples here. Academic scholars and other outside observers of the hippies have been cited as well, but use of their material has been sparing. The point of this volume is to present the distinctive ethics of the hippies on the hippies' own terms, from primary materials.

Writers for the underground papers were mostly male; for that reason, if for no other, this study is not perfectly representative of hippiedom, just as the underground papers are not. Also, the papers tended to lionize and publish the writings of certain countercultural celebrities. Works by and about Timothy Leary and Allen Ginsberg, to name perhaps the two most prominent examples, were published very frequently. Thus there may be an elitist tilt to this study, just as there was to the underground press.

The underground papers have been cited by date where possible. Where dates have been illegible or missing, citations have been made by volume and issue number. Obvious typographical errors have been corrected, but otherwise the material has not been altered; thus errors of usage and fact have not been corrected in quotations.

Chapter 1
The Ethics of Dope

Pursuing the religious life today without using psychedelic drugs is like studying astronomy with the naked eye because that's how they did it in the first century A.D., and besides, telescopes are unnatural.

—Timothy Leary, *The Politics of Ecstasy* (1968)

Smoke dope everywhere. . . . Dope is Great, it's fun, it's healthy. . . . Get every creature so stoned they can't stand the plastic shit of American culture. . . . Smoke dope, it's your duty to future generations, turn the world on, it's your duty to the universe.

—"Pun," *Other Scenes,* June 1968

Nothing else was so characteristic of the counterculture as dope. The overwhelming majority of hippies used it, and most who didn't approved of its use by others. The commitment to—as opposed to furtive use of—dope was the single largest symbol of the difference between counterculture and Establishment culture.

The use of the term "dope" here instead of "drugs" is deliberate. To the hippies, it served to draw a line between substances perceived to be good and those deemed bad. Dope was good; drugs, on the other hand, included both good and bad substances. The distinction was imprecise, of course. Hippies disagreed a great deal about where the line between good and bad should be drawn. Very generally, most hippies approved of such substances as marijuana, hashish, LSD, psilocybin, mescaline, peyote, and morning glory seeds. They were less approving, and often outspokenly critical, of amphetamines, methedrine, DMT, STP, barbiturates, the opiates, and sometimes cocaine. Psychedelics were good; speed and downers were bad. Substances that were perceived as expanding consciousness were good; things which made the user dumb were bad. A similar terminological distinction was made for merchandising: those who sold dope (and who used and valued it themselves) were *dealers;* those who sold drugs, the bad stuff, were *pushers.* But each individual made his or her own choices as to which substances fell into which category. There was no universally accepted dividing line between the two.

Tom Coffin was one hip writer who delineated the distinction between dope and drugs:

> We're talking about and doing Revolution, attack on all fronts, political, educational, religious, cultural, even *business. . . .* And dope is part of that revolution, and if you fear dope (Dope, not DRUGS—alcohol is a drug, pot is DOPE; nicotine is a DRUG, acid is DOPE; DRUGS turn you off, dull your senses, give you the strength to face another day in Death America, DOPE turns you on, heightens sensory awareness, sometimes twists them out of shape and you experience that too, gives you vision and clarity, necessary to create Life from Death) if you fear DOPE more than you fear Richard Nixon and his Machines Men of Death, then you have indeed sold out and bought in. . . . The difference between Stupor and Ecstasy is the difference between Jack Daniels and Orange Sunshine, between the Pentagon and Woodstock, between *The New York Times* and *Good Times.* We all have to make our choices.[1]

Usage in this chapter will follow this popular hippie perspective. "Dope" will be good and "drugs" bad, except that in some cases "drugs" will be inclusive of both types. I avoid those terms only in quotations, where the author's language stands.

Virtually everyone in the counterculture agreed that dope, whatever its correct name, was great. One all-star symposium sponsored by LEMAR International (the marijuana-legalization lobby), whose participants included Timothy Leary, Allen Ginsberg, Leslie Fiedler, Abbie Hoffman, and Jerry Rubin, "agreed that the biggest problem with drugs is shitty drug laws and the bad research."[2] The counterculture saw the main "drug problems" as spotty quality and high prices.

Dope was utterly intrinsic to the counterculture. The hippies believed that dope itself had altered the consciousness of millions of individuals in fundamental ways, and that that alteration was inevitably a major force in the establishment of the new culture. So contended Richard Alpert (later Ram Dass) when he wrote, "We've moved in the direction of a whole new model of the human brain. . . . You can travel anywhere, back into childhood, back through evolutionary history, cosmic history, down your own bloodstream or nervous system."[3] And it made the new culture sweet. As Jan Hodenfield wrote about the Woodstock festival in *Rolling Stone,* "Equal to the outside's anger and concern about the 'drug menace' was its awe at the 'politeness,' the 'good behavior,' the 'cheerfulness,' the 'lack of violence.' And the two were never connected."[4]

Dope, though good, was never seen as problem-free. What was important was that the downside was dwarfed by the upside. As Raymond Mungo wrote, "for us, everything is possible; if the heart is willing, what ecstatic adventure is too risky? *What is risk?*"[5]

So dope was a constitutive element of the counterculture. As Leary put it, "You have to learn the outside dope which is TV, and the inside dope which are drugs, and if you don't someone's going to do it for you and they're going to cop your mind completely. That's why your only hope is dope."[6]

From the perspective of several decades later, it is easy to observe that the hippies were overly optimistic about the power dope held for good, and often naive about the downside of drugs in general. However, the hippies enunciated an ethics of drugs that made more overall sense than any ethics or policies prevailing in the drug-hysterical years since, policies that have given us the enormously expensive but colossally futile "war on drugs." The main elements of the hip ethics of dope looked something like this: Use it positively. Use it sanely. Know what you're doing. Avoid bad drugs. Avoid misuse of (good) dope. Don't use dope to hurt others. Assert your freedom to make your own decisions about dope. And have a good trip.

The Spread of Dope

A UCLA professor was quoted in the days of hip as saying that "if a young man hasn't smoked pot by the time he's twenty, he's probably sick"—that is, "seriously neurotic"—because marijuana is "a way of life for America's youth."[7] Evidence from the hip era suggests that indeed huge numbers of the young were smoking it. A sample of 219 University of Kansas students in 1971 indicated that 69 percent had smoked marijuana and that 92 percent had friends who smoked it.[8] A 1971 Gallup Poll reportedly found that over 40 percent of college students had tried pot, a percentage "eight times as high as [that] recorded in a 1967 survey."[9] The College Poll found that in 1972, 60 percent of college students had used marijuana and noted that "the results of this annual drug study belie the theory that drug use on the campus is abating. It was generally thought that the drug culture was a unique one which would generally lose favor as the troubled era of the late 60s and early 1970s passed away. This now appears to be false."[10]

The National Commission on Marihuana and Drug Abuse, in its extensive survey published in 1972, found that twenty-four million Americans had smoked marijuana. The incidence of use reached 40 percent in the 18–21 age group, and 38 percent in the 22–25 age group.[11] Lewis Yablonsky, in a study that specifically focused on the counterculture in 1968, found that 90.7 percent of his sample had used marijuana and that 68.2 percent had used LSD.[12] All in all, dope achieved widespread use among youth in general, and it was the common denominator of the counterculture.

Massive increases in arrests and border seizures accompanied the spread of dope.[13] But neither stemmed the tide of dope. The *New York Times* estimated that 99 percent of the people at Woodstock were smoking marijuana, and a state police sergeant was quoted as commenting, "As far as I know, the narcotics guys are not arresting anybody for grass. If we did, there wouldn't be enough space in Sullivan County, or the next three counties, to put them in."[14] Many hippies believed that they were looking the future directly in the eye: "The drug revolution is with us, despite border shutdowns, surveillance techniques, police, everything. It's a revolution that's sweeping the world."[15]

Even before Woodstock, as early as 1967, hundreds could gather for smoke-ins without fear of arrest. Marijuana's sweet smoke permeated society. Even Kim Agnew, the daughter of the staunchly anti-dope vice-president Spiro Agnew, was busted in 1969.[16]

Something was happening, Mr. Jones. The psychoactive properties of marijuana had been known in the United States since the turn of the century, but the use of grass had spread only very slowly until the 1960s.[17] LSD and its unusual effects were discovered in 1938, and in the ensuing decades it was investigated as a tool for the treatment of drug and alcohol addiction, as well as a tool in America's clandestine Cold War struggles with the Soviet Union (the Central Intelligence Agency monitored early LSD research closely, seeing the chemical as a potential tool for espionage or perhaps for disabling a large enemy population).[18] Otherwise, however, LSD was hardly used until the middle 1960s, at which time it was still being sold legally.[19] With the emergence of the counterculture, however, marijuana quickly spread to the point that hippies could boast that it was "so widely used, it's unofficially legal."[20] And LSD wasn't far behind.

Why Hippies (and Others) Did Dope

Hip theoreticians had many explanations for the great surge of dope use. Three general points dominated the multifaceted debate: dope is fun, dope is revolutionary, and dope is good for body and soul.

Certainly fun was a part of it. The counterculture was unabashedly hedonistic. The hippie creed was "If it feels good, then do it so long as it doesn't hurt anyone else."[21] Hippies were perhaps the first to detect a social anomaly, that American society had seen an exponential growth in leisure time, yet was still basically suspect of fun for its own sake. A seventy-five-year-old hippie (!) commented upon being arrested that "in our culture it's wrong to do anything for pleasure. You have to have a higher motive. Well, I take it just because I like it. That's the only reason I would do anything. I don't do a thing under compulsion. And there's no reason to be ashamed of something I like. I say, God dammit, when I sleep with a woman or take a drink I'm not doing it for anybody. If I do it I do it for myself. So why not with everything else?"[22]

Yet there was usually a streak of rebellion in the pleasure ethic. The fact that fun was suspect was a reminder, the hippies argued, that Americans lived in cultural confinement and that the time had come for a social revolution. Dope was revolutionary because the larger society, which had learned to tolerate some types of deviant behavior, was utterly flabbergasted by this new challenge. Very quickly the use of dope became a cultural symbol, a means of thumbing one's nose at society. One counterculturist wrote, "People are taking drugs in repudiation of something—something most young people can see and understand, although we sometimes have a hard time defining it."[23] As a West Coast hip author concluded in 1969, "The government is right in its stand on drugs. They are a definite threat to society. . . . Drugs . . . must be ruthlessly suppressed lest the people feel too good."[24]

On the other hand, fun and rebellion were hardly the whole story. For many some of the time, and for some all of the time, dope was a tool that provided healing and insight. More than a few hippies claimed to have found through dope startling new insights and sometimes a comprehensive philosophy of life. As one wrote, drugs could be "related to the search for authentic human existence where a person is not alienated from himself and estranged from his fellow man and where God is more than a dead word. It is just possible that the drug scene is more closely tied to the province of existential questions of philosophy and theology than those of law or even medicine."[25]

Furthermore, American society demanded the spiritual search that dope seemed to enhance. Sensitive persons, counterculturists argued, had real trouble coexisting with the jive crap of American life—the race for money and status, the dehumanization that pervaded technological society. Dopers thus were Luddites who symbolically smashed the machines with their substances. A humanized society might not have required a chemical escape hatch. As hip author Tom Coffin put it, "were the real problems, of war and racism, alienation and anomie, poverty and pollution, to be solved (or even honestly worked on), the culturally-induced need for consciousness expanding drugs would be perhaps nil."[26] That was the point of Timothy Leary's frequent assertion that "Your only hope is dope." Leary's associate Richard Alpert, before he became Baba Ram Dass, similarly intoned, "We are not junkies, not in it just for kicks, nor are we sick. There is no category for us."[27]

Legalization

Although some theorists of hip argued seriously that dope needed to be illegal to maintain its revolutionary qualities, the vast majority, logically enough, supported legalization. As one wrote, "The issue isn't after all whether pot smoking is good or bad for us. The issue is how much longer and to what extent we can allow the state to control our minds."[28] Psychedelic guru Art Kleps agreed: "Your body is your own. If you don't own your own body, if you can't do what you wish with your own body short of hurting somebody else, then you're no better than a domestic animal."[29] In a similar vein, Stephen Gaskin, the leader of The Farm, one of the most prominent hip communes, promulgated this manifesto: "We believe that if a vegetable and an animal want to get together and can be heavier together than either one of them alone, it shouldn't be anybody else's business."[30] So basic was the issue that Allen Ginsberg once demanded a congressional investigation to find out just who was responsible for this "vast swindle" of illegal dope.[31] Wasn't freedom, after all, a paramount American value?

But there were always a few working the other side of the street. Some quite seriously believed that dope's value as a tool for challenging prevailing social values would be lost with legalization. Others argued that legalized dope would provide a windfall for capitalists, that an impersonal commercial dope industry would grow up, complete with advertising and high prices, and that such an industry would contradict the very essence of dope. Some simply argued that campaigning for what should be automatic was degrading: "Free men do not ask permission to enjoy their freedom."[32]

Some contended that dope should be legalized because it provided profound insights; others made a straightforward civil libertarian case for legalization. Still others, though, simply noted that the great increase in the use of dope that stemmed from the hippies' popularization of it made continued prohibition impractical. Comparisons were often made with failed prohibitions of the past, especially the classic American experiment with the prohibition of alcohol in the 1920s and 1930s. Howard Moody in 1972 listed several failed prohibitions: coffee drinking in the Near East in the seventeenth century, tobacco in sixteenth- and seventeenth-century Europe, marijuana in North Africa in the late 1950s, and the American prohibition of alcohol. Despite draconian penalties—capital punishment, in some cases—those efforts all failed.[33] So why not bite the legalization bullet?

The Dope Churches

The dope churches were a marvelously variegated countercultural phenomenon. Some evoked deep mystical religious experiences; others simply amounted to attempts to get around the drug laws. Some were deadly serious; some were whimsically lighthearted. Collectively they were one of the quainter byways of hip.[34]

The Native American Church, which predated the hippies by roughly half a century, was much admired by the hip-era dope churches. The Native American Church not only had a historic tradition of drug use for ritual purposes; it was the only place where a psychedelic substance, peyote, could be used legally. Many hippies were infatuated with Native American culture anyway, so the Native American Church fascinated serious hippie dopers. But the church was usually open only to ethnic American Indians, so the hippies were left to devise their own imitations of it.

No hip dope church, however, really resembled the Native American Church very much. For American Indians, the Native American Church was and is not primarily focused on getting high. Rather it is a way of getting in touch with ancient native traditions, of calling up through intricate and timeless rituals the wisdom of millennia of tribal culture. Peyote has always been one of several spiritual tools. Its use has been guided and controlled by elders whose spiritual experience has made them leaders. Hippies wanted to get high, and perhaps to see any vision that might be conjured up thereby. Native American Church members wanted to preserve and revive ancient traditions, including the visionary experience. Despite the large differences between hippies and Native Americans, however, the hippies genuinely admired and often imitated Indian ways, and some Indians felt affinity for the young dissenters who voluntarily placed themselves outside the oppressive social mainstream.

Within the counterculture the most "serious," in religious terms, dope church was Tim Leary's League for Spiritual Discovery. Leary wanted to avoid any organization at all for his psychedelic spirituality, keeping his religion "pure" and aloof from social structures. However, any use of dope meant challenging or evading the law, so Leary organized the League as an advocacy agency for chemical freedom.[35] As he described it, "We're not a religion in the sense of the Methodist Church seeking new adherents. We're a religion in the basic primeval sense of a tribe living together and centered around shared spiritual goals."[36] "In our religion the temple is the human body, the shrine is the home, and the congregation is a small group of family members and friends."[37]

The actual content of Leary's, and presumably therefore the League's, religion resembled some Hindu traditions, but the real point of having an organization was to push for the legalization of dope for sacramental, or at least spiritual, purposes. With the League came Leary's "Two Commandments for the Molecular Age": (1) Thou Shalt Not Alter the Consciousness of thy fellow man. (2) Thou Shalt Not Prevent thy fellow man from Altering his own consciousness.[38] The League was "dedicated to the ancient sacred sequence of turning-on, tuning-in and dropping-out. Its aim is to help create every man as God and every woman as Goddess."[39] Further, "We're saying the same thing Luther said to Rome: take the Bible and stand naked in your communication with God. Now the particular method we use is artificial. It shocked Rome when Luther said he could take this man-made thing and find God through it. He didn't need the apparatus of this enormous Church. It shocks Americans today when we say that anyone in a state of grace can take this chemical and stand naked before this Divine Process."[40]

Another psychedelic religious body was the Neo-American Church, headed by Chief Boo-Hoo (the name is deliberately silly; one shouldn't take oneself too seriously) Art Kleps. Kleps and Leary were friends and at one time mutual admirers, but their churches were largely dissimilar. Kleps explained the difference thus: "Leary has a religion; he is a spiritual leader. I am functioning like a pope who is nothing more than a super-business man."[41] Satire was the centerpiece of Neo-Americanism, whose logo featured a three-eyed toad and whose motto was "Victory over horseshit." Kleps contended that "the United States Government and all other churches are shared fantasies."[42] Was its chief attraction the possibility that sometime its members just might get legalized dope? "Yeah," answered Kleps, "I think that has a lot to do with it. And why not? The Catholic Church certainly doesn't hesitate to use all kinds of arguments of the same kind to seduce people into joining."[43] The Neo-American

Church had religiosity mixed with cynicism, satire, and lack of respect for propriety, all of which renders the group hard to characterize easily. And characterization is more difficult than ever once the inquirer has read the group's special scripture, *The Boo-Hoo Bible*, certainly a product of nonlinear thinking.[44]

A much more "serious" organization, and one that stood essentially apart from the counterculture, was the Church of the Awakening. Founded by John Aiken, a retired physician, in 1963, it advocated the use of dope "as an aid to meditation," and thus was interested in the legalization of dope, but at the same time tried to keep a middle-class orientation. If Kleps represented the left wing of psychedelic religion, the Church of the Awakening represented the right. Its religious concern was entirely serious. As Aiken said, implicitly disparaging other dope churches, "We're not there just to promote the use of psychedelics."[45]

Beyond these prominent groups there were several other psychedelic churches, most of which seem to have been short-lived. Among them were the Shiva Fellowship Church, the Psychedelic Venus Church, the Fellowship of the Clear Light, the American Council of Internal Divinity, and the Psychedelic Peace Fellowship.[46] They ranged from relatively conservative (along the lines of the Church of the Awakening) to absurd (some groups appear to have been more whimsy than religion), but all shared a basic desire to legitimize the psychedelic religious experience.

Beneath the dope churches lay serious concern for the right of individuals to use dope, especially for religious purposes, without interference from any outside source. All professed a libertarian attitude toward dope, and all argued that dope was more than just fun, that it was a true sacrament.

Few hippies argued that dope *couldn't* be used as a sacrament, but some were nevertheless skeptical of psychedelic religiosity. Some politicos complained that heavily religious use of dope led to the pursuit of spiritual experience at the expense of social concern and activism. A more common complaint was that the religionists were sometimes narrow in that they tended to restrict dope to the religious sphere and deny its secular usefulness as fun or escapism.[47] However, the critics generally agreed that dope churches pointed up a legitimate concern for internal freedom, and thus were a valuable part of the counterculture.

The Ethical Case for Dope

Hippies didn't just tolerate dope; they said people *should* use it. Counterculturists argued that dope was distinctly useful to just about anyone in several specific ways.

Dope as a means of understanding and coping with the evils of American culture

As symptom, dope use reflected dissatisfaction with the prevailing culture. But the hippies saw it as much more than just a symptom. Dope, it was argued, could enhance that dissatisfaction by clarifying one's understanding of the great errors of Establishment society. As some hippies put it, dope made people understand the cultural disease on the cellular, as opposed to the intellectual, level. The individual then had to choose between dropping out of that culture as nearly as possible or trying to remain within it, but with a perspective that made it bearable, a perspective involving a certain detachment that said that life could be lived fully even within a generally meaningless culture—with, of course, the help of insights gained with the aid of dope. An anonymous hippie wrote in 1970, "If nothing else can be said for marijuana, it can be praised as a cultural detoxicant; it acts as an emotional detergent that breaks through the sham and hypocrisy and living-death of much of contemporary America, and allows that vision of beauty that American life seems so bent on destroying."[48]

Ram Dass (then Richard Alpert) once said that the role of dope was "quite simply to upset the apple cart."[49] And there was value in that upsetting: "Drugs break patterns, that's all they do. When patterns are broken, new worlds can emerge."[50] With the psychedelics, value systems changed. People became more aware than before of their social conditioning and more interested in overcoming that conditioning to live lives based on choice rather than inevitability.

Some key insights were said to come while one was high, but they carried over to life in general, and thus dope was critical because it was held to form the basis of an entirely new way of thinking. Moreover, it was widely believed that once a person came to this new way of thinking, and consequently living, he or she would have trouble reverting to former patterns. Dope, the hippies argued, engendered a profound revolution in consciousness. Most countercul-turists agreed with Will Albert that this revolution would have an "ultimately beneficial effect on our society."[51] It showed the way out of the rat race to a more comfortable, relaxing, and meaningful way of life.

Dope and religious experience

So many hippies believed dope was in some way productive of religious experience that a bibliography of such contentions would run to many pages.[52] In general, it was held that dope could be a key to individual religious experience, that it could help a given religious community to cohere, and that it could affect the lives of users in such a way as to effect ethical action (or at least to promote a particular ethical outlook on life). Such claims were supported in many cases by references to other (traditional) cultures in which the use of dope for religious purposes has long been accepted (as in the case of the peyote- and mushroom-related religions in the Americas and elsewhere).

In such religious esteem was dope held that many spoke of it as a sacrament and contended that it should be used ritually, as would befit a powerful substance: "A sacrament is a covenant between man and God and also any ritual that corporately grows out of that covenant to express it more fully. It can be bread and wine, peyote or mushrooms, a cup of tea, LSD, the tobacco used in the sacred pipe, whatever is put into the body to connect the world outside with the world within."[53] This sort of sentiment was fairly common, even if most counterculturists did not go as far as Tim Leary did and assert that dope should be used *only* as a sacrament.

To most, dope was not *exclusively* a path to ultimate religious truth, even if providing spiritual experiences was one of its functions.[54] And that it was a new sacrament did not make it inherently suspect. Indeed, newness gave it a special validity and a special urgency: "Sacraments wear out. They become part of the . . . game. Treasure LSD while it still works. In 15 years it will be tame, socialized routine."[55] Or, as the Boston mystic Mel Lyman wrote, "LSD does what alcohol did when IT was new and what EVERY new creation does, it lets a little more light into the darkness of man. It is art, it is philosophy, it is education, it is whatever fills the mind with more light. . . . It is a trip from the mind to the soul and back again, a ROUND trip."[56]

Not all of the counterculture considered the use of dope a predominantly religious experience, however. In a rather unscientific survey called "Black Market Research," conducted by underground papers in New York, Dallas, and Detroit, 38 percent of the respondents in both New York and Dallas said that their use of dope was at least sometimes religious, while in Detroit the figure was 87 percent.[57] There were a few who believed dope would not lead one to deep religious conviction (Paul Krassner once said that LSD provided "a different God that I didn't believe in"), or whose concerns regarding dope simply fell a long way from anything that should be called "religious."[58] (Two of the most important early apostles of LSD, after all, had very different approaches to the matter of psychedelic religion. Ken Kesey and his secular Merry Pranksters used LSD to have an outrageously good time, while Timothy Leary and the psychedelic religionists were deeply serious in their religious explorations.) Still, the belief that dope had religious potential was widespread. Leary cited five specific studies as collectively having indicated "that (1) if the setting is supportive but not spiritual, between 40 to [sic] 75 per cent of psychedelic subjects will report intense and life-changing religious experiences; and that (2) if the set and setting are supportive and spiritual, then from 40 to 90 per cent of the experiences will be revelatory and mystico-religious."[59]

R. E. L. Masters and Jean Houston determined that 96 percent of the 207 subjects in an experiment seeking to describe the content of dope-related religious visions experienced visual religious imagery of some kind.[60] Walter Houston Clark, a veteran psychedelic researcher in the Boston area, went even further, stating, on the basis of 100 replies to a questionnaire circulated among users of psychedelics, that "so far there is *not one* who has not described some element of religious experience on the questionnaire," and going on to describe many specific testimonies of religious experiences from previously nonreligious individuals.[61] Many countercultural writers agreed with that sort of finding. Even though there was virtually no critical analysis of such religiosity, the fact that people experienced it was widely affirmed. Testimonies to that effect were legion. This one was provided by an unidentified writer in the *Washington Free Press:* "Most of those who have used LSD report that through this drug they have found a spiritual agility and a gracefulness which leads them to believe they have achieved an unusual unification of the mind, the soul and the senses. They also seem to believe that the psychedelic drugs can give them special insight into themselves."[62]

That religious experience could be related to at least some drug experiences would appear to have been demonstrated by Walter N. Pahnke in his "Good Friday" study, in which psilocybin was administered to several volunteers, and a placebo to others, in a double-blind experiment in Boston. The experiment took place in the basement of a chapel on Good Friday. The sound of a worship service upstairs was piped in for the volunteers. Employing standard categories that scholars have used to describe the religious experience, Pahnke concluded that those taking the psychedelic chemical had substantially more profound experiences than those receiving the placebo.[63]

The relative lack of analysis of the nature of the psychedelic religious experience by underground writers is problematic. Such analysis as was offered was nearly always analogical, generally comparing psychedelic religious experience to some more conventional religious experience, most frequently to Asian religious traditions. Episcopal Bishop James Pike, speaking to a hip audience, contended that the psychedelic and mystical experiences were "identical," since monks fasting, for example, "create chemical changes through vitamin deficiency that lifts the screen the same way that the drug lifts the screen."[64]

Among underground writers, some saw dope as a shortcut to true mysticism (it was said to be capable of "stripping off the sludge which has accumulated on us").[65] Others saw it not as a shortcut, but as a discipline by which one had a chance to explore new sequences of goals.[66] Whatever the nature of the experience, though, there was a very widespread agreement that it was real: "What's phenomenal about LSD and related mind-changers is that drug technology hasn't just brought us delirium or flashing, fascinating entertainment; it has actually given us something akin to the philosopher's stone. It has discovered a way to mass-produce extreme experience."[67]

Dope was not only seen as important for individual religious experiences, but also as useful for fostering religious community. William C. Shepherd observed that the ritual use of dope produced a very important "sense of social 'belongingness.'"[68] Willie Minzey, the leader of the Shiva Fellowship of the Neo-American Church in San Francisco, saw the religious element of dope best manifested in the concept of Shiva, which he said was revealed "thru joyous group spiritual experience involving the use of psychedelic substances."[69] A hip commune-dweller wrote of LSD, "We use it as a sacrament within our family structure. . . . We don't take it to ball, to freak out, or trip out. We use it specifically to keep ourselves together."[70] The rituals surrounding dope provided a new basis for group intimacy, and dope itself helped maintain and further that intimacy, its users believed.

Dope religion usually stopped with mystical experience, but in a few cases it produced in the partaker an ethical imperative. Several countercultural writers maintained that dope was the direct cause (or one direct cause, at least) of the concern in the counterculture for ethical action. Underground papers proclaimed that "some have discovered LOVE through dope,"[71] and as a result "feel as Messiahs, . . . eager to spread their message of salvation from an essentially irreligious, non-humanistic and unesthetic society."[72] And, as in other situations, dope's carryover effect worked here: the ethical insights inspired by dope remained when the high was gone. "Many have noted the tendency of psychedelic users to make major life-changing decisions while under the drug, decisions that are often carried through once the drug wears off," P. G. Stafford noted. Dope gave the user the "opportunity for 'self-transcendence,'" and that phenomenon could, at least in some cases, result in ethical concern and activity.[73]

It should be noted in passing that both scholars and underground writers were well aware that drug-related religious experience has solid historical precedent. In addition to the use of dope in Indian, American Indian, and other cultures, some saw dope in the Judeo-Christian tradition.[74] Thaddeus and Rita Ashby speculated that peyote may have been among the "vegetables" mentioned in Romans 14:2 and elsewhere.[75] Reading the hip writers, one is reminded of John Allegro's contention that mushrooms were the basis of the Judeo-Christian tradition—indeed, that "Christ" was simply the secret name for the sacred fungus.[76]

But the past here was less important than the present. Quite simply, as one writer put it, "The psychedelic movement is, for me, a holy thing, and it is for a lot of people who are into it."[77]

Awareness of nature and one's unity with it

In several instances underground writers advocated the use of dope as a means of communing with nature and understanding the natural order of the world. Nature meant the whole environment, urban as well as rural. As "Paul Scorpio" wrote, "A stone on the curb of my street didn't mean the same to me as a stone in the middle of a forest; it was important to consider the totality: sound, light, absence of human beings, how the stone got there and where it might be tomorrow or ten years from then, etc."[78]

This sense of wonder at nature was connected to the appreciation many hippies cultivated for Native Americans. It was also related to the urgency many hippies felt in wanting to preserve the world's environment. Persons were part of the natural world, and feeling and appreciating that was part of the dope experience.

Dope and better sex

Many hip writers valued dope for its alleged heightening of sexual pleasure. The LSD experience was often described as resembling sexual experience in its sensuousness; but beyond that many believed that dope was a splendid aphrodisiac. Timothy Leary, in a celebrated *Playboy* interview in 1968, made an extravagant version of the claim:

> The three inevitable goals of the LSD session are to discover and make love with God, to discover and make love with yourself, and to discover and make love with a woman. . . . The LSD session that does not involve an ultimate merging with a person of the opposite sex really isn't complete. . . . One of the great purposes of an LSD session is sexual union.
>
> It's socially dangerous enough to say that LSD helps you find divinity and helps you discover yourself. You're already in trouble when you say that. But then if you announce that the psychedelic experience is basically a SEXUAL experience, you're asking to bring the whole middle-class monolith down on your head.[79]

Leary's claim may have been overstated, but the perceived relation of dope and sex in the counterculture was supported by the Black Market Research studies. Seventy percent of the Dallas respondents, 33 percent of those in New

York, and an unspecified "high" percentage of both male and female respondents in Detroit said that they engaged in sex while turned on with dope.[80]

That any form of dope is an aphrodisiac is debatable from a scientific point of view, but insofar as dope (especially marijuana) tends to create in its users a sense of relaxation and social intimacy, it certainly has the potential to enhance sexual pleasure. In addition, most dope expands the user's perceived sensory awareness, which could logically lead to an increase in experienced sexual pleasure. Marijuana often distorts the user's sense of time and thus can give a sense of prolonged orgasm.[81] Whatever the biochemical facts, most hippies were convinced that dope could and did enhance sexuality and pleasure.

Dope can heighten intimacy, interpersonal interaction, and cooperation

Dope was held to promote a sense of intimacy with the social world just as it did with the natural world. William Braden saw the counterculture as departing from the metaphysical dualism that for centuries had fostered privatism and individualism. The counterculture, even though it had cultural conflicts with other elements of society, came to maintain that although persons had individual minds and beings, they were nonetheless all related.[82]

Some countercultural writers saw dope as a key to bridging deep cultural chasms. "The new force unleashed by LSD constituted the primary unifying factor in a grouping which ranged from the sometimes violent Hells Angels motorcycle club to meditating Zen Buddhists," two Philadelphia writers contended.[83] Another writer saw this unity graphically demonstrated in a marijuana smoke-in in New York: "Psychedelic technology really works, not just as a way to get high, but at the very least, as a way of diminishing friction between people. And, after all the talk of psychedelic revolution, the real, shared experience of the smoke-in contributed to something that all the money or media coverage hippies can marshal couldn't insure. There is peace in the park. If the psychedelic revolution involves even this minimal social transformation, then it has to appeal, in an immediate and living way, to the socio-economic groups that stand to gain through social transformation."[84]

But the community engendered by dope tended to extend only to the initiated. Indeed, that community was by and large at odds with the rest of society: "Drugs leave a feeling of being different from anyone else who does not use drugs and a brotherhood, if only chemical, with those that do."[85] Nonetheless, communal solidarity was part of the overall dope experience. Some believed that the community setting of hippiedom prevented addiction; it was the lonely, the outcasts, for whom use turned into abuse and compulsion.[86]

Dope as a neutral tool

The majority of counterculturists argued that dope itself was positive and pro-ductive of beneficial experiences, that it both had intrinsic power for good and was used in such a fashion (that is, in supportive groups, for the most part) as to promote positive reactions. A minority of hippies argued, however, that dope was neither good nor bad of itself. It took on meaning and value only as it was used, and the drug's actual role in the overall experience could be seen as quite limited. Andrew Weil has summed up this line of thought well by speaking of dope as an "active placebo" in which the effect is substantially supplied by the user.[87]

Timothy Leary presented a variation on this argument in contending that LSD merely served to assist the user beyond his or her "imprinting," which was a "biochemical event" by which the greater portion of the brain was ren-dered inaccessible.[88] With his colleagues Ralph Metzner and Richard Alpert he wrote, "Of course, the drug does not produce the transcendent experience. It merely acts as a chemical key—it opens the mind, frees the nervous system of its ordinary patterns and structures. The nature of the experience depends almost entirely on set and setting."[89]

"Set" meant the preparation of the user, in terms of personality struc-ture and mood at the time. "Setting" meant the environment: the physical surroundings (weather, the atmosphere of the place involved), the social en-vironment (feelings of persons present toward each other), and the cultural environment (the "prevailing views as to what is real").[90]

In this view the value and benefit of dope is supplied by the user. "It's like fucking, or eating potatoes, or anything else. There are people that hurt them-selves using it, and there are people who are better for using it."[91]

Just fun: dope makes you feel good

One simple but important argument for the use of dope was that dope was fun. It makes you feel good, the argument went, both while you are high and afterward. As one hip writer put it, "The holiest, happiest, healthiest people I know are those who have used the most dope."[92]

The Black Market Research studies indicated that most dope users saw fun as a major part of it all. Ninety percent of the Dallas sample, 51 percent of the New York sample, and an unspecified "high" percentage of the Detroit sample confirmed that having fun was a part of their dope experience.[93] In fact, the studies themselves were criticized by one writer because they attempted to make a semiscientific determination of the ideology of dope, which was con-trary to its spirit: "The way of life, for a whole lot of smokers, is just to get high."[94]

The pleasure ethic was not held in especially high esteem in American society in hippie days, at least theoretically, because it conflicted with the Protestant work ethic.[95] So the counterculturists again clashed with the values of the prevailing society. The watchword of the counterculture was "If it feels good, then do it so long as it doesn't hurt anyone else." According to the hippies, dope, per se, really didn't hurt anyone, and certainly it did not do direct damage to the nonuser. Bad trips were rare, given attention to set and setting. It was nonusers rather than users who were concerned about them. Most of the damage that dope did to society, said the hippies, was caused by oppressive drug laws, not by dope itself. Thus the counterculture believed that pleasure was a perfectly legitimate reason for using dope.

Dope is harmless

The counterculture not only maintained that dope was socially harmless, but also that it was not dangerous to the normal person—or at least not more dangerous than the drugs with which society was generally infatuated—namely, nicotine, alcohol, amphetamines, and barbiturates. Andrew Weil, in his early book *The Natural Mind*, which was widely read by hippies in the 1970s, claimed that virtually every human society ever known has used some kind of agent to alter consciousness: "In fact, to my knowledge, the only people lacking a traditional intoxicant are the Eskimos, who had the misfortune to be unable to grow anything and had to wait for white men to bring them alcohol."[96] If we are destined to use drugs anyway, why not use a less harmful rather than a more harmful substance?

The Black Market Research studies indicated that 84 percent of Dallas respondents and 73 percent of New York respondents had never experienced undesirable aftereffects, or hangovers, from dope.[97] During the heyday of hip a number of physicians and scientists affirmed the relative harmlessness of dope in articles widely printed in the underground press.[98] At least one, the widely read "Dr. Hippocrates" (Eugene Schoenfeld), argued that the notion that LSD was harmful was a distorted idea promoted "by those who oppose new ideas out of fear, ignorance and prejudice. The LSD controversy may well be remembered in history as ranking with the persecution of those who thought the earth was round or that the universe did not really move about the earth."[99] In sum, the hippies believed that a cocktail party was a cesspool far worse than a hip festival, and Grey Line tours were "vastly more deadening and sterile than an LSD trip."[100]

The medical usefulness of dope

The goodness of dope was underscored by its medical potential. When hippies began to use dope, some medical researchers were already convinced that it was useful for the treatment of some mental disorders and, in the case of LSD, treatment of alcoholism.[101]

Enough therapists believed in the clinical usefulness of LSD that in the 1960s they founded the Society of Acid Therapists. Essentially, LSD therapy attempted to help an individual through his or her problems by stripping away the learned perceptual framework that was acquired in the maturation process. In the case of alcoholism, underground press articles often cited scholarly literature which suggested that in some cases LSD apparently helped cure the disease.[102] Marijuana also was held to be useful for various health problems. A Liberation News Service story in 1970 described Army studies that indicated that marijuana might be useful medicine for victims of tetanus, migraine, high blood pressure, and sunstroke.[103] Later it became fairly well accepted that marijuana was useful for the relief of glaucoma. Was there anything dope couldn't do? Several decades after the heyday of hip, over a dozen states have legalized marijuana for medical purposes. The hip tendency to regard dope as a panacea has, at least to some extent, been vindicated.

Dope and creativity

A key countercultural claim for dope was that it was a great wellspring of creative ideas and action. Writers, musicians, and graphic artists saw dope as inspiring, or even creating, their art. Everyday hippies, as well as professional artists, subscribed to that point of view. In the Black Market Research studies, 54 percent of the Dallas sample, 25 percent of the New York sample, and an unspecified "high" percentage of the Detroit sample indicated that they pursued creative work while high.[104]

Much of that creativity was believed to come directly from the dope high, but perhaps even more was attributed to dope's carryover effect, the sense that insights gained while high influenced, positively, later activities. So asserted Allen Ginsberg, arguably the foremost countercultural figure in the arts: marijuana, for example, was "a useful catalyst for specific optical and aural aesthetic perceptions."[105] He continued, "Drugs were useful for exploring perception, sense perception, and exploring different possibilities and modes of consciousness . . . and useful for composing, sometimes, while under the influence. Part II of 'Howl' was written under the influence of peyote. . . . 'Kaddish' was written with amphetamine injections."[106] Most hippie artists did not produce works as powerful as Ginsberg's, but they enthusiastically shared his belief in the creative powers of dope.

Countercultural Opposition to Dope and Drugs

Despite their general infatuation with dope, many counterculturists saw that the larger drug world did have a downside. There were, indeed, harmful drugs; good drugs/dope could be used in a destructive manner; and, worse, there were a few unscrupulous souls around who would use dope for evil purposes, especially for controlling others.

Opposition to harmful drugs and to abuse of dope

Despite the popular perception that hippies were indiscriminate dopeheads, the counterculture regarded most drugs as harmful, without substantial redeeming social or personal importance. They destroyed the good that dope had done; they sundered rather than improved the fabric of society. Almost invariably both heroin and the amphetamines were seen thus; alcohol was sometimes included. Tim Leary saw dangerous drugs as the main reason for the fiasco that was the Altamont concert of December 1969 (a large California Rolling Stones concert at which one person was murdered): "I think it's of great Psycho-pharmacological interest that the drugs which were most obviously on display at Altamont, particularly around the bandstand were not Psychedelic Drugs but Speed, Smack, and Booze."[107]

One hip writer contended that "speed and smack will change your mental attitude. . . . The moment you stick a point in your arm you have unnaturally altered your whole life."[108] Yet in the case of heroin, the real culprit was often seen as the federal government and those who kept heavy drugs illegal, since they unwittingly promoted the crime in the streets that results from illegal heroin.[109] Allen Ginsberg once accused the Narcotics Bureau of actually promoting heroin, since it meant more appropriations and more jobs within the Bureau. Moreover, strong anti-marijuana campaigns, such as the ill-fated Operation Intercept, a Nixon administration program devoted to intercepting marijuana at the border, usually resulted in a massive increase of heroin use, resultant crime, and death by overdose.[110]

Many hip authors condemned amphetamines vigorously. Timothy Leary: "Amphetamines, all of them . . . get you on the wrong track on the way to your energy source. . . . Speed is the symbol of an unturned-on world of growling machinery."[111] Allen Ginsberg: We need a "general declaration . . . contra speed-amos. . . . Speed is anti-social paranoid making, it's a drag, bad for your body, bad for your mind . . . a plague on the whole dope industry."[112] David Faber: "Everything about speed is cheap, neon, plastic, ugly Amerika."[113] The warnings were frequent in the underground press. The staff of *Dallas Notes* deemed the problem worthy of a special "Speed Issue" devoted to condemning it.[114]

Many other substances were also considered harmful, and therefore to be condemned, by the underground. In case after case, the underground papers warned readers of bad substances to be avoided, from cocaine to Hawaiian wood rose.

How exotic did weird highs get? The *Spokane Natural* once took note of accounts in the popular press that hippies were injecting themselves with such strange substances as peanut butter, Aqua Velva, Right Guard deodorant, pizza sauce, oil from unhydrogenated peanut butter, mayonnaise, and a brew made from freeze-dried coffee. Such stories, maintained the *Natural,* were simply put-ons:

> NO ONE IS STUPID ENOUGH TO DO IT.... It's an old head joke. And the heads have been putting on the police so well that it's become a national "new fact."
>
> In all due respect, the police have been the victim of a tremendous hoax.... It's the old "big lie" technique—tell a small lie, and it will be disproved, but tell a big lie and everyone will be so overwhelmed that he'll have no choice but to believe it.
>
> And that's the whole point of this article—that ignorant people will believe anything because they don't know enough to refute it.... Because [the police] believe that every marijuana user "graduates" to heroin, they have no trouble believing that people really shoot-up peanut butter.[115]

Even good dope was considered subject to misuse. One had to keep one's perspective. Allen Ginsberg again: "Too many people are taking too many chemicals.... There seems to be an entire class of people who take too much of everything. It is like overeating. Acid is really harmless but if you keep taking it too often you have so many different visions of so many different universes you never integrate them."[116] And some dope was bad because on the street it could be impure: "The major medical problem with acid at the present time is quality control."[117] So the counterculture favored the use, but not the abuse, of dope, and condemned other drugs. For, after all, "That drugs are on occasion misused (i.e., abused) does not significantly detract from their potential benefits."[118]

Opposition to using drugs to influence others

In the early, formative days of the counterculture, Ken Kesey and his Merry Pranksters performed a number of "acid tests" in which LSD was dissolved in punch that, it became widely believed, people drank without knowing of the presence of the chemical. (Kesey later claimed that he never dosed anyone without due notice.[119]) At the time there was little public countercultural opposition to such practices (indeed, at that time the counterculture hardly existed), but later such activities came to be roundly condemned as, in Tim Leary's words, contrary to "the number one commandment in our religion: Nobody has a right to change my consciousness, I have no right to change your consciousness."[120] When acid testing without notice to partakers occurred at a Los Angeles Easter Sunday Love-In in 1968, Art Kunkin, the publisher of the *Free Press,* felt compelled to denounce it, writing, "Turning people on without their knowledge and consent is violating the privacy of another person's body and mind."[121]

In several cases the counterculture saw flashes of what Allen Ginsberg called "a chemical dictatorship."[122] The most prominent case was that of the Charles Manson family, in which drugs were allegedly constantly used as a means of social control.[123] And even though the counterculture disclaimed Manson, saying that he had not "had anything at all to do with the hippie culture,"[124] the inevitable fact was that other would-be Mansons were always nearby, willing and able to prey on the weak.[125] Ed Sanders, in his book on Manson, dwelt at some length on several pain/fear/drug groups that, he said, influenced and controlled more than a few people.[126] Some claimed that a similar phenomenon developed in a group that arose in Boston around Mel Lyman, whose *Avatar* was among the most mystical and cosmic of the underground newspapers. Lyman was given to making spiritually grandiose statements, even going so far in his paper as to claim to be "Christ appearing in this modern day and age."[127] *Rolling Stone,* in a special series of articles, attacked the Lyman group as potentially more dangerous than the Manson family.[128] Members of the Lyman Family, as it has generally been called, were not always pristine (some were involved in an attempted bank robbery in 1973, among other things), but the *Rolling Stone* allegations surely seem exaggerated. After all, the Lyman Family is still together, and its members are productive citizens in several locations across the country. (Mel himself is said to have died in 1978.)

And countercultural journalists told other tales of alleged acid fascism as well. Lucian Truscott told of a huge party near Aspen in 1970 at which a woman, about fifty years of age, was encouraging people to drink her punch, which was "alive with acid," apparently gathering them for some sinister purpose under her "complete control."[129] Separating truth from fiction in these anecdotes is difficult, but the countercultural bottom line was clear: one had the right to control the expansion or alteration of his or her own consciousness without impediment of law, and there could be nothing but total condemnation of those who would commit the most serious drug abuse of all, using drugs to influence others.

Total opposition to dope and drugs

Dope was part of the very definition of the counterculture, but there were some individuals and groups related to the hippies who, for various reasons, opposed drugs, including dope, entirely. The most common basis for the opposition was religious. Followers of Meher Baba, for example, hip in many ways, frequently opposed the use of dope, claiming that drugs did not give truly new insights, as good religion did, and tended to enhance the ego,[130] or that they helped to perpetuate the illusion that material reality actually existed.[131] (Meher Baba taught that there was no reality except God. One might well ask why drugs mattered at all, since they did not exist.) Most of the Indian gurus admired by hippies similarly opposed all drugs. Swami Satchidananda, for example, reasoned that since it was harder to become a holy person than a doctor or a lawyer, "how can there be a pill to make a man holy when there is no pill to make a doctor or lawyer?"[132]

The counterculture overwhelmingly rejected such thinking, of course. Allen Ginsberg dryly observed, following an argument with the Maharishi Mahesh Yogi, that LSD was actually the key to the Maharishi's success in America, since trippers enlightened by LSD were those open to his message, and that, at any rate, no matter what the gurus said, the religious value of LSD was utterly obvious to a great many persons.[133]

The other main locus of opposition to all use of dope was the New Left, some of whose activists saw dope as incompatible with the coming revolution. Dope drew persons inward, removing them "from the arena of social consciousness and collective struggle."[134] One writer described the New Left's scornful initial reaction to the rise of dope use as "bread and circuses, the ultimate pacification program."[135]

Still others opposed dope for a variety of reasons. Some believed that an adequate high depended on one's state of mind and could be achieved without dope. David Crosby—ironically, considering his own later history of dependency—once noted that the popular Indian musician Ravi Shankar was always stoned but never used dope.[136]

And others simply found dope a waste of time: "And so you get stoned and grin and giggle and waste away the most joyful, alive years of your life. Talking about drugs, where to get them, how much, how good, who's been busted—never speaking of 'heavy' real things, like nature, art, each other, ecstasy."[137]

Still others saw dope as a product of capitalism, and therefore a product to be avoided if possible. One writer described the "drug hierarchy" as "one of the most capitalistic enterprises to be found anywhere," its customers exploited by "a cruel machine which sneers at revolution as it rakes in profits."[138]

But these arguments were as straws in the wind. The counterculture as a whole loved dope, its psychic staff of life. The few hippies who rejected dope were not influential. Nonhippies who tried to make the case against dope were regarded as either lamentable or vicious. When Mike Curb, the young president of MGM records, in 1970 dropped eighteen groups that "advocate and exploit drugs" and encouraged radio stations to refrain from playing songs "with drug-oriented lyrics," *Rolling Stone* denounced his action as a "sick grandstand stunt." It also noted that Curb did not cut his best group, Eric Burdon and War, which was selling a lot of records. Steve Gold, Burdon's manager, replied, "Isn't that the sickest pile of bullshit you ever heard? . . . This must be the last dying gasp of a man that's failed and is on the way out. . . . We're a drug-oriented act and have never tried to hide that."[139]

Chapter 2
The Ethics of Sex

Take off your clothes, unless you're cold, and touch each other—yes, even strangers. Make love—not to one guy or chick who you grab onto and possess out of fear and loneliness—but to all beautiful people, all sexes, all ages.

—Ron Norman, *Seventy-Nine Cent Spread,*
November 5, 1968

We do not announce the "sex orgy." We announce the true spirit of the high holy act of fucking. People must be free to fuck without molestation, without fear, without guilt.

—"Om," *Berkeley Barb,* June 5–11, 1970

In its use of dope the counterculture proclaimed freedom of access to mental pleasure. Sex did the same for physical pleasure: free people should express their sexuality as they choose. To the hippies, any special character that sex might have did not mean that it should be restricted. Sex was, rather, a range of powerful and wonderful feelings and activities that one should feel free to enjoy at will. No person was to be forced to engage in any sexual activity, but neither was any person required to restrain his or her sexual impulses. Sex was good. Sex was fun. Sex was healthy. And this hip approach to sex helped revolutionize attitudes and practices in the nation as a whole.

A note from the introduction needs to be repeated here: the heyday of hip came before the widespread dissemination of contemporary feminist thought, and some hip writing on sex looks, several decades later, distinctly unenlightened. Sex roles were often traditional in the counterculture, and when feminist ideas first began to be raised in progressive circles, around 1968, many male hippies turned out to be as disinclined to give women equal rights and privileges as males elsewhere in society.[1] A fair number of the early new feminists were influenced by the counterculture. One could argue that they tended to take seriously the talk of equality that heretofore had been conceived in class and racial terms, and perhaps the gap between expansive hippie rhetoric and the disinclination of many hip males to liberate themselves from old sexual thinking helped some spur new feminists into revolt.

In any event, sexual liberation was presented in the underground press in largely male-oriented terms. The point of the sexual "revolution" was, disproportionately, male pleasure. The counterculture bloomed before either contemporary feminism or homosexual activism amounted to much. *Roe vs. Wade* was still years down the road as well, and devastating disease was not much in the picture (yes, there were sexually transmitted diseases, but the common ones were easily curable). Many former hippies reading their old utterances on sexual liberation would probably put things differently today.

The Broad Case for Liberated Sexuality

The concept of free sexuality is hardly new. Its advocates have run from the ancients through such phenomena as the "complex marriage" of the Oneida Community and the larger free-love movement in the nineteenth century to more recent advocates of sexual liberty such as Albert Ellis.

Sex, in the counterculture, was fun and free, certainly more fun to engage in than to write about. "Anyone who has time to write articles protesting sexual mores should fuck more," one hip author intoned.[2] At the same time, sex was understood as an expression of humanness, a means of human communication that operated at the deepest levels of being. It was the "human touch, without conquest or domination, and it obviates self-consciousness and embarrassed speech."[3] As Leah Fritz of Berkeley wrote, "As for sex—like eating, like walking in fresh air, like all human activity—it should recreate us, help us to find one another, make us real, and tangible as the earth. It should put us together again, body and soul, male and female, in harmonious intercourse."[4] Pleasure and communication, then, were the two main touchstones of countercultural sexuality. To a lesser degree, sex was also held to be revolutionary.[5] As one countercultural author put it,

Sexual repression is counter-revolutionary. It is the denial of our most basic self. When sex is both repressed and sublimated it is the driving force of civilization. "Don't let those slaves fuck around, man, we've got a pyramid to build."

Fortunately, as we all know, civilization is teetering on the brink.[6]

The hippies were in the vanguard of a revolutionary smashing of sexual taboos. Concern over promiscuity, opposition to masturbation, demanding that sex be strictly marital, and guilt feelings over being sexually active have clearly decreased sharply in American culture as a whole over the last several decades, and the hippies were among the first to occupy the turf of sexual liberation.

What was once known as promiscuity was widespread in the counterculture, but it was no longer shameful or hidden. Now it was time to redefine terms. "Don't apply descriptions of promiscuity to yourself. It's the first step toward involving yourself in endless attempts to prove those tags as self-definitive. And that's a pile of bull-shit, lover, you don't deserve to bear."[7]

The counterculture saw the marital contract as irrelevant to sex. "A legal contract for a sexual relationship is, if not out of date, at least beside the point for most of us."[8] Some went further, maintaining that sexually exclusive marriage itself was a manifestation of what was wrong with Western sexuality. As a countercultural writer in Seattle put it, "There is no reason why [sex] should not be shared. It not only brings you closer to your friends but it also brings you closer to your wife or husband. The concerned Christian I am sure would not believe this; but consider the Eskimos; they were invariably described as the happiest people on the earth until we gave them "virtue." Now they too have chastity and adultery and jealousy. Instead of happiness they are as glum as the concerned Christians and with the same hang-ups."[9] Guilt over one's noncoercive sexual activities was declared out-of-bounds:

> There are people, young and old, who enjoy their own sexuality and enjoy sharing sex, with no guilt feelings. They like their bodies. They like other people's bodies. They are not self-conscious of *bodies* . . . they are not *afraid* to express themselves when they want to.
>
> It is *great* to make love and not feel guilty about it.[10]

Since "there is no activity which is in itself sick,"[11] countercultural condemnation of any voluntary sexual act was hard to find. The *Village Voice,* for example, gave space to advocates of sadism and masochism as well as to those of asexuality and virginity.[12]

Some favored masturbation. "Masturbation is not something to do just when you don't have a lover. It's different from, not inferior to, sex for two."[13] And "honest masturbation is a lot healthier than a dishonest lay."[14] Others liked transvestism.[15] Homosexuality was entirely acceptable. Group sex and sexual party games? No problem.[16] The hip credo ruled the world of sex: If it feels good, do it, as long as it doesn't hurt anyone else.[17]

But liberated sexuality in the counterculture went beyond the simple level of freedom of choice and orgasmic gratification. Some argued that sex was far more than simple copulation, that regarding sex simply as an act of ejaculation was symptomatic of the "sensual sterility in the Western culture."[18] A higher ideal was that of total sexuality in which, as Don H. Somerville put it, there were several reproductive organs but only one sex organ—the whole body.[19] Quite a few hippies became interested in the writings of Wilhelm Reich, who promoted a "complete" orgasm that released tension and gave pleasure throughout the body.[20]

Homosexuality

One of the most important components of the hip-era sexual revolution was the rise of public gay consciousness, and the underground press gave considerable publicity and support to that phenomenon. Although one cannot exactly argue that the hippies spawned the gay liberation movement, it is fair to say that hip tolerance of sexual activity contributed to the atmosphere in which the gay revolution could emerge.

Homosexuals and their supporters wrote frequently in the underground press, making a broadly based case for an ethics of homosexuality.[21] Their arguments were not unlike those of the heterosexual liberationists. There were five main lines of argument:

1. *Homosexuality is natural and good.* "To deny the rightful existence of homosexuality is a perversion of the laws of nature. . . . People are capable of being gratified sexually by any person. . . . To limit sexual contact to male-female genital play is dumb."[22] Many writers noted that there have been many times and places in history in which homosexuality was not only accepted, but even preferred. The ancient Greeks had a proverb, a hip writer averred: "For children a woman, for true love, a boy."[23] Some pointed out that homosexuality could provide an essential social service to an overpopulated world, since it inherently involved total birth control.[24] It also helped reform—for the better—sex roles, offering an alternative to the "present patriarchal patterns of male-female heterosexuality."[25]

2. *A person has a right to free sexual choice.* Although relatively few hippies said that homosexuality was the *only* good sex, it was a choice as legitimate as any other. While "the whole world is not gay," as one wrote, hippies stood for nothing if not freedom of choice.[26]

3. *One should not have to hide his or her sexual preferences.* Homosexuality wasn't wrong, and it shouldn't have to be secret. Gays needed to "stop mimicking straights; stop censoring ourselves."[27] "Our message is that homosexual love is good. Holding hands is not inappropriate."[28] It was in the spirit of openness that one group of California homosexuals devised a short-lived plan to take over Alpine County, a sparsely populated piece of the Sierra Nevada, in 1970. Why should there not be an openly gay junior college, a gay museum, gay housing, gay health services, gay public officials, gay publications? Homosexuals should have the freedom that others have to live openly and to construct their own social environment when and as they choose.[29]

4. *All private acts between consenting adults should be legal.*[30] Why was it that two men could get into a boxing ring and hurt each other with people watching, but not have private love? Why was oral copulation illegal? "Blow jobs are beautiful. They are natural, basic, simple, fun. . . . Something so important as that . . . should be legalized."[31]

5. *Social discrimination against homosexuals should end.* Under social conditions then prevailing, homosexuals were not only subject to occasional unprovoked physical attacks, but also restricted seriously in security clearance, military service, citizenship, and employment, among other things. Homosexuals paid taxes, said a gay Texan, but "the only things we get for our taxation are undesirable discharges and bad employment records when we are discovered in government jobs. Local banks will accept homosexual money but fire homosexual employees. Oil companies like homosexuals to have credit cards but dislike giving them paychecks."[32] As Supreme Court Justice William O. Douglas was reported to have written, "Homosexuals have, in this century, been members of both Congress and the Executive, and have served with distinction."[33] It was time, according to the counterculture, to legitimize free sexual preference. In sum, "All we hell-raising homosexuals want is humanness. And we will have humanness when every man understands he is more similar to than different from his fellowmen and is willing to contribute a little effort to insure the same quality of life for everyone in the community."[34]

When a militant new phase of the gay rights movement took shape in the wake of a police raid on the Stonewall bar in Greenwich Village, New York City, in June 1969, the new revolutionaries found a sympathetic audience among the hippies and often a soapbox in the underground press. A few weeks after the Stonewall raid, for example, the *New York Rat* approvingly reported the formation of the Gay Liberation Front and announced the platform of the new militancy: "We are a revolutionary homosexual group of men and women formed with the realization that complete sexual liberation for all people cannot come about unless existing social institutions are abolished. . . . We are creating new social forms and relations, that is, relations based upon brotherhood, cooperation, human love, and uninhibited sexuality. Babylon has forced us to commit ourselves to one thing . . . revolution."[35]

Nudity

Nudity was part of the counterculture's new sexuality. The public was first made widely aware of countercultural nudity by the Woodstock festival, whose press reports rather luridly featured mass skinny-dipping, but the phenomenon was more pervasive than that. In part the counterculture simply revived classic nudist philosophy, which argued that clothes hindered interpersonal communication, that going without clothing was natural, and that nudity was just plain fun. But the counterculture generally stopped about there, rejecting "establishment" nudism's emphasis on physical exercise and proscription of public sexuality in the nudist context.

Graphic representation of nudity was a prominent part of the underground press. Photos of naked women and men were common, and underground cartoons contained depictions of nudity that ranged from the explicit to the depraved. The underground comic books ("comix") were often fixated on sex and nudity, determined to smash the prevailing society's taboos so vigorously that in a fair number of cases they had little redeeming social importance.

Nudity was in keeping with the counterculture's love of bodily pleasure, and as such it was not so much exhibitionism and voyeurism as it was appreciation of the total body. In fact, countercultural nudity proposed to liberate persons, through overexposure, from excessive concern with genitalia. As a hip writer put it,

> It is in the interest of any culture to perpetuate a special excitement on the part of its members in the genitals. The propaganda runs that "real sexuality" exists finally in the groin. . . . The genitals are judged to be ugly [and therefore distinguished] from the rest of the body which is potentially beautiful and so not particularly sexual. . . . Had the genitals been left uncovered

they would have blended naturally with the rest of the body. . . . All parts of all healthy bodies would have been equally well suited for pleasure. . . . Thus . . . every unveiling of the genitals to public inspection will upset the limiting fixation that the genitals are somehow each person's own piece of ugly private property. Similarly, every revelation of the genitals will disturb the esthetic cop-out away from the need to get pretty in the eye before one can get warm in the groin. (The various sensory mixtures that will result include getting pretty in the groin and warm in the eye.) When the genitals lose their special significance then people will cease to fear them and so cease to need to build special monuments to them. It is because they are hidden that they are ugly and dirty.[36]

Where did the countercultural passion for nudity originate? LeRoy Moore Jr. argued that it all began with the civil rights demonstrations in which the physical importance of bodies for strategic purposes was stressed: "This tactic of bodily presence spread to a multitude of causes and a variety of forms ranging from passive nonviolence to provocative convulsions born of frustration and despair. But in every case the effect has been to provide by means of a bothersome presence of bodies a tangible witness of value (or disvalue) of particular bodies and public rebuke for those who victimize the body."[37] A different case might be made for the influence of *Playboy,* which a decade before the beginnings of the counterculture had broken the taboo in an openly available publication. Although the counterculture generally derided the plastic nudity of an airbrushed Playmate, *Playboy* nonetheless made the important innovation of taking nudity and sex out of the closet. It placed (male) sexual pleasure in a context of fashionable middle-class living and, by filling the magazine otherwise with good works of fiction and nonfiction, implicitly said that nudity and a concern for bodily pleasure were not incompatible with the workings of the mind. Many hippies criticized *Playboy*'s exploitation of women, but to a fair degree it was the counterculture that put *Playboy* founder Hugh Hefner's theories into practice. Although by the latter days of the counterculture the emerging feminist critique was pointing out the bias and exploitation of the *Playboy* approach, the magazine's role in the development of countercultural sexual ethics is inescapable.

The counterculture's advocacy of nudity, as of liberated sexuality generally, rested primarily on grounds of fun and freedom: nudity was fun per se, and it was a symbol of the lifestyle freedom advocated by hippies. It wasn't an end in itself, nor was it a therapeutic tool, as it was in certain encounter groups. It was, rather, a simple enjoyment of a given time and place. In the words of LeRoy Moore Jr., hip nudity said, "Here I am; see me; so what is new?" It extolled "a loss of a certain sense of shame, accompanied by a sense of wonder and playfulness."[38] Thus one underground writer could say,

> Nudity on a beach, meadow or forest is an experience that is very much apart from sexuality. It is a communion with all of the gods' creations. It is a pure animal delight in the freedom of the body wildly playing in the elements. It is an aesthetic joy in the beauty of the human form. It is one of life's richest and most pleasurable experiences. . . .
>
> This growth is heartening in a world of silly hang-ups. Nudity makes one free of hang-ups. One becomes a part of the wind and water, and once this is experienced one can never wear a bathingsuit again.[39]

Furthermore, nudity was held to stand for the sort of freedom that should be basic in a free society: "If I have any liberty at all, I have the liberty to be naked. . . . If the State shall deny me this right, then it may deny me any other right it sees fit."[40]

The fact that nudity was a cultural taboo meant that it could provide a vehicle for dissent. Sometimes the dissent was generalized, as in the case of public nude-ins.[41] Nudity outraged the majority of citizens, and that was reason enough for it. As Richard Neville, a staunch proponent of uninhibited sexuality, wrote, it "communicates a commitment to total rehabilitation of social values, it makes news, and surprisingly discourages arrest."[42] So mass nudity provided a vehicle for collective nose-thumbing at society. That was the sort of feeling that Louis Abolafia tapped when he appeared at nude-ins around the country in 1968, running as the naked candidate for president on the slogan "What have I got to hide?"

But nudity as dissent could also be more specific than that. In some cases, hip mothers stripped their children to keep them out of public schools.[43] In a well-publicized incident at Grinnell College, six women and four men undressed in the presence of a representative of *Playboy* to protest that magazine's exploitation of the female body. ("Playboy Magazine is a money-changer in the temple of the body. Playboy substitutes fetishism for honest appreciation of the endless variety of human forms.")[44] The Shiva Fellowship, which held many nude meetings in public parks in San Francisco, advocated "immediate nudity as resistance to hostile cops at public demonstrations."[45] Indeed, there were many proposals for confrontational nudity (most of which never materialized), sponsored by such groups as the Neo-naked Noisy Committee for Peace and Love and the Bare Breasts for Peace Brigade. In a manner reminiscent of the Doukhobors, Canadian religious sectarians some of whose members have taken off their clothes as an act of defiance at times of conflict with the government, the hippies found that nudity can interfere effectively with the usual procedures of the civil authorities.

Sacramental/Symbolic/Ritual Uses of Sex

Although the predominant attitude toward sex in the counterculture was supportive of sexual freedom on grounds of pleasure and individual free choice,[46] there were some who saw liberated sexuality as having a larger significance. Free sex and nudity could lead to a "feeling of communion," to an exhilaration that "is such that it comes close to supernaturalism."[47]

One movement for liberated, sacramental sex was the Om United Nude Brigade. Richard Thorne, a former president of the Sexual Freedom League, proclaimed that he was "the living personification of Om, who is . . . the creator of the universe,"[48] and had manifested himself "to announce universal nudity and the holiness of copulation. . . . We must abstain from selfishness, jealousy, possessiveness, but not copulation."[49] The Brigade came to public attention in a series of public marches, in which Thorne's followers paraded in the nude. It claimed divine authority: "If dicks are lewd, if pussies are obscene, then God is lewd; God is obscene. For it is God who made the dick to fit the pussy; God who made the pussy to fit the dick."[50]

Another group which decorated its sexual thinking with religious trappings was the Shiva Fellowship (and its successor, the Psychedelic Venus Church), which held many public nude meetings, several of which resulted in arrests.[51] One of its "rituals" was oral sex, which it called a "genital sacrifice."[52]

Some even argued for sacramental sex in traditional religious settings. After all, had there not once been ritual prostitution in the Temple in Jerusalem? One Gay Liberation Front member writing in the *Berkeley Tribe* described a spontaneous male homosexual act on an altar, quoting one of the participants:

> I began making love to him, kissing his cock and balls all over. Then I went down on his beautiful cock with my mouth and tongue working it.
>
> Then I felt him come. I really felt it, and tasted it. I've never felt closer in sex than I did at that moment. There was a high mystical energy level. . . .
>
> It was much more meaningful to drink the sweet juice of a human being than the juice of a grape at the altar.

And the other participant in this particular act concurred in its religious significance: "I had mixed feelings about it, even while Steve and I were having sex. But, as it continued, I realized that this was the highest form of worship and felt good about it."[53]

The Revolution's Limits: Real-World Concerns

Although the counterculture generally approached sex from a point of view of fun and individual free choice, mundane reality was never far away: not everyone wanted sex to be whimsical, and things like diseases and birth control were parts of the equation that one ignored at one's peril.

The case against the clap

One result of the sexual revolution was the spread of sexually transmitted diseases to near-epidemic proportions.[54] The clap (a common nickname for gonorrhea, the most pervasive sexually transmitted disease of the era) was, as one writer put it, "one of the hangups of the new morality."[55] The counterculture's reaction to the problem did not involve any renunciation of free and widespread sex, but generally reflected the obvious wisdom that pertained to it: get treatment immediately, tell any person who might be infected, and take reasonable precautionary measures where possible. Cooperating with public health officials in this case was eminently reasonable. "Don't think fink! You're doing your friends a favor. It's the only way to stop the spread of the disease."[56]

The case for sex with love

A new sexual era or no, some counterculturists still found sex best within a context of love and concern for the partner. Sex was less than ideal, these persons said, when it was engaged in casually, without real concern for the other person, or under the outdated system of male domination and female submission.[57]

Timothy Leary called into question the whole matter of labeling widespread, uninhibited sexual contact "sexual freedom":

> I think . . . that what's called "sexual freedom" in the United States (which goes along with promiscuity) is just a reaction to Puritan heritages and is not a way of life that's going to stand up as spiritually centered. Infidelity, of course, occurs in large cities and capitals of empires, for when there's boredom, when the spiritual thread has been lost, then you find what you had in Babylon and in Rome and in Athens. Promiscuity can only exist in a city. . . . In a small tribal community the challenge and also the necessity is to make it within the stable relationship, and then you find that the whole thing is within one woman anyway.

> [Promiscuity is] an ideal to which all of us honestly respond. I think it
> takes a tremendously high level of consciousness to pull that off, and there
> is an incredible opportunity here for cop-outs and for egocentricity and for
> dishonesty.[58]

So in the quest for a new sexual ethic, some tempered absolute freedom: sex
in the meaningful context of love could be better than sex that was casual and
transitory.

Birth control and abortion

Birth control was an obvious necessity in the world of liberated sexuality. Thus
the hip literature on the subject mainly discussed relative efficacy and safety
of various methods, not the rightness or wrongness of birth control itself.[59]

Abortion was not quite so clear-cut. The counterculture flourished before
the Supreme Court's *Roe v. Wade* decision legalizing most abortions. Abortion
was then regulated by the states and was widely illegal in most circumstances.
Generally, abortion was regarded as the most logical solution to unwanted
pregnancy, but the hippies, like just about everyone else, found it the least attractive form of birth control. Advocacy of freedom of choice prevailed, and
by December 1968, a female counterculturist writing in *Buffalo Chip* was out-
lining what soon became the position of the nascent women's movement: a
woman's body is her own, and she should be free to obtain an abortion when
she wishes to.[60]

The founding of the National Association for the Repeal of Abortion Laws
in 1969 got favorable reviews in the underground press. In September of that
year the *New York Rat* published a cover story that provided a detailed guide
to getting an abortion despite the prevalence of generally restrictive laws—re-
minding readers, however, that "no matter how relaxed you feel about having
to face an abortion, it's still a really shitty hassle and more expensive than
you can easily afford."[61] Within a few months the critique of the status quo on
abortion was becoming more polished and incisive. A *Rat* piece by the Wom-
en's Liberation Health Collective related some illegal-abortion horror stories
and proposed a program for reform—research on the best and safest abortion
methods, making abortions available without charge, and so forth.[62]

A minority of counterculturists, however, resisted free choice. (In what
was perhaps a portent for the future of the abortion debate, most of the hip
writers who announced their demurral from the choice position were male.)
Ken Kesey was one who supported abortion only to save the life of the mother,
arguing that society needed to care about everyone, including "the un-dead
old [and] the un-born young." As he put it, "Abortions are a terrible karmic

bummer."[63] Similarly Stephen Gaskin, the founder and leader of The Farm, the archetypal hippie commune in Tennessee, was so opposed to abortion that for years The Farm had a standing offer: "Hey Ladies! Don't have an abortion, come to the Farm and we'll deliver your baby and take care of it, and if you ever decide you want it back, you can have it." A pregnant woman could go to The Farm, receive room, board, and health care, have the baby delivered, leave the baby at The Farm if she chose to, and still be free to reclaim the child at any future date—all without charge.[64] For Kesey, Gaskin, and the minority they represented, the single fabric of life was not to be torn.

Orgies and Organized Free Sex

Although for most hippies liberated sex remained a one-on-one (at a time) experience, another minority argued that orgies had a place in the new sexuality. One writer argued that orgies provided an outlet for the "non-ordinary sexual inclinations which we all possess," that orgies were harmless, that they helped to break down social barriers, that they helped create community spirit, that they were beneficial to one's private sex life, and that they were revolutionary.[65]

Most hippies did not condemn orgies, but neither were they attracted to organized sex, since the hip spirit of liberated sex was one of spontaneity, not sex with as many partners as possible. Many hip authors criticized organized, impersonal "swinging," which they identified as a manifestation of middle-class shallowness, conduct utterly inferior to the caring relationships, or at least honest pleasure, the counterculture advocated.

But the line between personal liberated sexuality and orgies could be hard to draw. The Sexual Freedom League (SFL) embodied the ambiguity. It had been founded with a hip orientation, scorning "double standards between the sexes, . . . out-dated sex laws on the books, and the continuance of hypocritical morality and diseducation on the subject of sex."[66] In its early days the SFL expressed a desire to "spread new ideas and living concepts" and "to have fun."[67] "The Sexual Freedom League puts a large emphasis on pleasure NOW, but we feel that if pleasure is the end product of the sexually free society, it is also legitimate to insist on our prerogatives to enjoy that pleasure now."[68]

Although the SFL was founded in hippie spontaneity, it quickly attracted followers from outside the counterculture, and its orientation shifted somewhat as a result. It became Establishmentarian—indeed, it became SFL, Inc.—and became hung up on sexual frequency and technique, concepts that were hardly spontaneous. Sex in the SFL ultimately became boring, to the point that some of its members decided that "screwing isn't what they want all the time. Many men at parties are getting a thrill just cuddling with the women."[69] By then, however, most hippies were gone from the SFL. Organized free sex was usually not the countercultural way.

Sex and Dope

Sex was the essence of one of the hip arguments for dope, as we have seen: dope was good because, among other things, it enhanced sexual experience. Over and over again the countercultural writers saw sex and dope as synergistic. Dope helped persons expand their erotic horizons, to realize that lovemaking did not consist of orgasm alone. Timothy Leary summed up the dope/sex connection thus: "The key energy in our revolution is erotic. . . . The sexual revolution is not just part of the atmosphere of freedom that is generating with the kids. I think it is the center of it. The reason the psychedelic drugs, particularly marijuana, are so popular, is because they turn on the body. I'll say flatly that the meaning and central issue of the psychedelic experiences is erotic exhilaration."[70]

Opposition to Liberated Sexuality, Especially When Focused on Male Pleasure

There was always a loyal minority on sexual issues among the hippies. The most frequent critiques came from the emerging women's movement, some of whose advocates saw freewheeling sexual relationships simply as an extension of the male-dominated sexuality of American society at large. The most extreme position in the late 1960s came from SCUM, the Society for Cutting Up Men, whose manifesto, written by Valerie Solanas, began, "Life in this society being, at best, an utter bore and no aspect of society being at all relevant to women, there remains to civic-minded, responsible, thrill-seeking females only to overthrow the government, eliminate the money system, institute a complete automation and destroy the male sex."[71]

But many rhetorically more moderate women simply advocated withdrawing from the sexual revolution insofar as it involved masculine predominance. "Free" sexuality, like any other kind, "carries with it an unwarranted domination by the man, of the woman, which injures both,"[72] a hip southern female wrote. Another woman was more blunt: "The talk of love is profuse but the quality of relationships is otherwise. . . . The idea of sexual liberation for the woman means she is not so much free to fuck as to get fucked over. . . . Our mothers could get a home and security, a prostitute—money, but a hippie woman is bereft of all that."[73] So some simply felt a need to withdraw from the sexual revolution until the social framework for heterosexual relationships was changed for the better.

It was at about this time that lesbianism gradually entered public discussion. The argument was simple and direct: it was difficult to find a truly liberated male who treated his partner "as a HUMAN BEING, not just a piece of meat. This is virtually impossible in our society," and therefore the alternative was female homosexuality, which "eliminates the necessity of tolerating male chauvinism in our lives without giving up the need for meaningful love relations."[74] "Isn't love between equals healthier than sucking up to an oppressor?"[75]

All of this was new and tentative in hippie days, as the women's movement was just beginning to gather steam. By 1968 the phrase "Women's Liberation Movement" was beginning to appear in the underground press as well as in the larger society. Late that year the New York Rat covered a feminist demonstration staged by the radical group WITCH (Women's International Terrorist Conspiracy from Hell), whose marchers exorcised money from the financial district and protested exploitive sexually oriented entertainment in downtown New York.[76] Hippies were slow to become enlightened, but probably not more so than any other major group in society. Indeed, hip openness about sex probably contributed importantly to the discussion—to the fact that lesbianism, for example, could now be talked about publicly. As late as 1970 it was still only in the underground press that the general public could read a lesbian's speculation that "maybe after the revolution, people will be able to love each other regardless of skin color, ethnic origin, occupation, or type of genitals."[77]

As I have argued above, hip culture itself played an important role in the rise of the new feminism. Much of the early feminist press in the late 1960s had distinctly countercultural graphics, makeup, and rhetorical tone. There was, for example, a clearly countercultural sauciness to Everywoman, a Los Angeles feminist paper founded in May 1970, and given to running articles with titles like "Hymens for Husbands."[78] Hip topics were addressed from a feminist perspective in many of the feminist papers, as in a Baltimore paper's article "Women and Rock: Sexism Set to Music."[79]

In one bold move, an entire major underground paper suddenly went feminist. On January 24, 1970, a group of militant women, some of them staffers of the paper, occupied the offices of and took over the New York Rat, announcing that "the culture has got to be revolutionary as surely as the revolution has got to be cultural."[80] The first issue under the new management contained "Goodbye to All That," a manifesto by Robin Morgan that was reprinted many times elsewhere—Abe Peck, who provided a good chronicle of the takeover, called her essay "the shot heard round the Left"[81]—and thereafter the paper was run permanently by the women's collective, dropping the previously broad cultural side of its coverage in favor of radical feminism and New Left politics generally. Morgan's polemic set the tone: "Goodbye to Hip Culture and the so-called Sexual Revolution, which has functioned toward women's freedom as did the Reconstruction toward former slaves—reinstituted oppression by another name."[82]

Feminism and women's concerns were not the only sticks in the spokes of the sexual revolution. Sexual liberationist Jefferson Fuck Poland wrote of three other anti-free-sex influences: what he termed religious fanaticism, especially that of the Hare Krishnas, whose movement was nearly celibate; heroin use ("Junkies rarely ball, unless for cash to buy junk. Heroin provides an orgasmic feeling of its own while suppressing sexual desire"); and methedrine use ("While speed doesn't always eliminate sex, it often does so"). Poland theorized that this antisexuality came from "ten years of failure in the Movement for peace, love and racial brotherhood," which had made many former true believers bitter cynics who rejected loving relationships and, as part of the process, turned to mysticism, violence, or antisexual drugs.[83]

Some argued that the sexual revolution was itself antisexual, at least in its more extreme phases. Tom Hayden once castigated the *Berkeley Barb* and, by extension, other aggressively free-sex underground papers as being decadent rather than liberated: "The Barb only appears to make a break with these repressive [sexual] patterns. There is a sexual attitude in the Barb which seems to suppose that whatever is taboo in America should be celebrated by radicals. But there is such a thing as sexual decadence which should be uninteresting, while not being taboo, to radicals. The Barb reveals this decadence in its sexual focus. The Barb represents a hip version of the morality of the Dirty Old Man, rather than exploring real alternatives to America's sexual neurosis."[84] Another hip author saw the new sexuality as actually only an increasing narcissism that was really a new and extreme Victorianism in which physical requirements for sexual partners became increasingly exacting. Sex ceased to be pursued for its own sake; it was sought for ego inflation.[85]

Those who had reservations about uninhibited sexuality, however, were a decided minority. Underground writing as a whole put if-it-feels-good-do-it sex up in the pantheon alongside peace, love, dope, and rock and roll.

Chapter 3
The Ethics of Rock

Rock music is one of the most exciting phenomena of our times. At its best in concert it is complete synesthesia, combining all of the arts and appealing to several levels of appreciation at once—emotional, intellectual, physical and metaphysical.

—Ron Jarvis, *Space City!*
January 17–30, 1970

Sound, like sex and the magic weeds, is a turn-on.

—Tom Sayles, *East Village Other,*
August 19–September 1, 1967

Rock and roll was as integral to the counterculture as dope and sex. Rock swayed a generation both physically and emotionally. The hippies lived and breathed it and believed that it was the most important new musical form to come along in centuries. As Chester Anderson put it, rock "engages the entire sensorium, appealing to the intelligence with no interference from the intellect. Extremely typographic people are unable to experience it."[1]

The point of this chapter is not to analyze the appeal of rock to a generation of American youth, but to look at the ways in which the music influenced the feelings and behavior of its devotees, and to see why hippies regarded a musical genre as pivotal to the generational rebellion. Insofar as this chapter is rational, it will, the hippies would have said, miss dealing with the real power of rock, since the music was preeminently something to be experienced and could not be explained entirely rationally. To the hippies, rock was not just sound; it was part and parcel of a way of life. Its ethical dimensions were therefore substantial.

The underground press during the flowering of hip focused overwhelmingly on rock, but folk music was also important to the countercultural musical scene. Folk was the music of cultural rebellion until around 1966 or even later, when the Beatles began to take on mythic significance as interpreters of the culture, new specifically hip rock bands (the Grateful Dead, for example) began to appear, and Bob Dylan incorporated rock into his previously folkish music. Earlier 1960s folk music (Joan Baez, Dylan) continued to be played on hippie stereos. The counterculture had little sense of history, so many hippies undoubtedly were not concerned with the folk roots of their music. But certainly the folk revival of the 1950s and early 1960s cultivated the ground for the advent of rock.

The protest music of Pete Seeger, Phil Ochs, and a host of others was full of peace and justice themes as well as loaded with distrust of the cultural and political Establishment. As rock historian Geoffrey Stokes has pointed out, folk was a critical catalyst for sixties rock because it bridged the musical gap between the fifties and the sixties: the originally pioneering, revolutionary rock of the fifties had given way by the early sixties to musical styles represented by the likes of the Beach Boys (catchy but formulaic), on one hand, and Andy Williams (smooth but utterly unchallenging and reminiscent of the music of the hippies' parents' generation), on the other. "Faced with the choice between teen and treacle," Stokes writes, "a lot of young people turned to folk music."[2] And from the energized folk scene major portions of the new rock emerged.

Rock as a Cultural Language

Dope usually involved inward experiences; liberated sex in most cases involved interpersonal relationships on a one-to-one basis. Rock, however, was communal, and thus it provided a medium for cultural communication. "Rock music," Ron Jarvis wrote, "is responsible more than any other single factor in spreading the good news. For joy and ecstasy is the essence of rock."[3] Media philosopher Marshall McLuhan, whose ideas circulated widely in the counterculture, reminded us that in our time the content of communication could not be separated from its means of propagation, and that went in spades for rock.

Rock and roll is the music of RIGHT NOW, every minute, pounding and screaming at your head, twisting inside your belly, pulling you up off your ass to GIVE IT UP and let energy flow through your cells and into the air so you can be FREE again.[4]

People need music to live. We believe that and act on it, all ways. Only straight people—honkies—think music is superfluous, that it doesn't make any difference what you listen to, and their lives demonstrate their ignorance. Music shapes us and makes us whole, as we would never be without it. We have to have it. There's no way you can get around it. For our generation music is the most vital force in most of our lives.[5]

Several features of rock set it apart from other types of music, thus effecting its power. The most basic feature was its incessant rhythm, the driving 4/4 beat. That rhythm demanded dancing, so rock was physical. Rock was sexual. Concerts always featured sensuous dress and performances on the part of both musicians and fans. High amplification was part of the whole, and so were the lyrics that, as with any successful vocal music, expressed the values and concerns of their listeners.

Most counterculturists, however, had no time for even such simple bits of analysis. Rock was a totality, one infused with power. Rock fueled the cultural revolution because it was immediate, spontaneous (at least to the listener), and total. The fact that the lyrics carried a message wasn't the central point.[6] One could dance to it, but "it doesn't care about the artificiality of merely being heard," one hip writer wrote. Countercultural icon John Sinclair got to the heart of things: "Rock and roll is the great liberating force of our time. Its most beautiful aspect is that it gets to millions of people every day, telling them that they can dance and sing and holler and scream and FEEL GOOD even when they have to listen to all those jive commercials and death news reports all around the music, everything's gonna be all right as soon as EVERYBODY GIVES IT UP!"[7]

Some hip analysts tried to figure out just where that power came from. Chester Anderson, for example, suggested that bass notes were experienced as localized vibrations in the abdomen; that rock rhythms affected the heart, skeletal muscles, and motor nerves; that long, open chords lowered the blood pressure, while crisp, repeated ones raised it; and that melodies affected the larynx, which autonomously subvocalized with rock lyrics.[8]

Most hippies, however, were content to let it be.

Rock, of course, used modern technological equipment, which made it something of a countercultural paradox—after all, wasn't this a back-to-basics, simple-living movement? The answer had to be that rock transcended its technology and merchandising, that the spiritual guidance of rock was independent of state-of-the-art equipment. Rock was more than the sum of its electronic parts. The danger always lurked that it might become "too rational, too business-like, and too orderly," given its merchandising.[9] But rock had the inherent power to overcome the limitations that such a structure might place on it. Indeed, without such power it wouldn't have been *rock,* but just noise.[10]

Rock and Dope

Charles Reich argued in his best-selling *The Greening of America* that dope was "an integral part of the musical experience," and he found little argument among counterculturists.[11] Certainly the conjunction of drugs and music was nothing new under the sun. Jazz musicians, for example, were using various drugs, from marijuana to heroin, for decades before the hippies appeared. Thus the counterculture simply expanded on its musical heritage when it created acid rock, music which was intimately related to cherished dope.

After the Beatles' *Sgt. Pepper,* the seminal album of acid rock, rock and dope could not be separated. For public consumption, most musicians, for quotation, had to deny that music and dope were interrelated, but the truth was closer to Beatles drummer Ringo Starr's comment that dope "made a lot of difference to the type of music and the words," providing new musical styles and new subject matter for lyrics.[12]

Part of dope's impact on rock was realized through its influence on composers and musicians, but just as important was its influence on listeners, who of course determine what will survive in the marketplace. Listening to music high wasn't the same as listening to the same music straight. Music with a special clarity and resonance to a substance-affected mind would triumph, and did. Dope's carryover effect was held to be operative here as elsewhere. Dopers tended to follow up in everyday life the experiences and insights that came through a high, so the music that was so wonderful when one was stoned was the music one listened to the rest of the time as well. But beyond that, rock spoke to the realities of life of the era—it spoke "about being yourself, about the terror of [contemporary] life, about the need for love. . . . In listening to such music when high—when the message really gets through—it's more difficult to evade these matters," wrote P. G. Stafford in the *Chicago Seed.*[13]

Rock and Revolution

Underground theorists frequently asserted that rock was revolutionary, although there was no consensus about what that meant. For some, it meant that rock could be used by political revolutionaries in much the same way that country-and-western music has long been used at political rallies by conservative neo-populists, especially in the South. A few rock bands were avowedly revolutionary in intent. The Detroit group MC5, for example, announced in 1969 that it was "totally committed to the revolution," and its manager, John Sinclair, was given a draconian dope-related prison sentence presumably because of his revolutionary politics. Still, some hippies were skeptics. Ron Jarvis called revolutionary rock "extremely naive and wrong-headed. . . . Music, like the other arts, is anarchic—defying all categories yet paradoxically including them all."[14]

The larger revolutionary role for rock lay outside specifically political arenas. It lay in the purported ability of rock to expose the sham of Western culture and to change the life orientation, political and otherwise, of its listeners. That is the sense in which Jonathan Eisen labeled rock "profoundly subversive."[15] Revolution, that is, could be defined otherwise than as direct political confrontation. Country Joe McDonald, who vaulted to fame at the Woodstock festival, noted that "one of the most revolutionary things you can do in this country today is to have a good time and enjoy yourself."[16] Or, as an anonymous writer put it, one shouldn't see "things like music (or whatever) as frivolous to the revolution. Shit, if the revolution is not about our own lives and getting high and smashing the state and getting in touch with ourselves and each other, then it ain't no revolution."[17]

The idea that music has extraordinary potency is hardly a new one. Plato had Socrates remarking to Glaucon in the *Republic* that "musical training is powerful, because rhythm and harmony sink deeply into the soul and fix themselves there solidly."[18] The elder theorist of hip Ralph Gleason preached the cultural revolutionary power of rock by quoting the seventeenth-century Scot Andrew Fletcher of Saltoun, "Give me the making of the songs of a nation and I care not who makes its laws."[19] Gleason argued that "rock music in America has been the single most potent social force for change for several years now,"[20] and "that is why Dylan seems to me to be more important than the Weathermen. They blow buildings in New York. He blew minds all over the world. Ginsberg's poems speak to more people than all the SDS pamphlets put together."[21] As a counterculturist wrote to Abbie Hoffman after he had tried to disrupt the Woodstock festival to make a political point, "Fuck your rhetoric, man . . . it's more fun to dance and sing than fight [and] it's gonna change a lot more heads."[22]

So rock was the revolutionary ultimate. Fundamentalist Christians to the contrary, one writer asserted, "we all know what's going to eventually save the world. Rock, that's what."[23] But there was always an uncomfortable underside to all that. Rock was inevitably commercialized, partly because the equipment and production expenses for it were high, and bills had to be paid. Some hip commentators, therefore, said rock was inherently compromised and couldn't be counted on as the vehicle of the revolution.

Common sentiment to the contrary, Irwin Silber, a key catalyst in the folk-music revival of the 1950s and early 1960s, argued that the Beatles, Bob Dylan, the Rolling Stones, and even the Fugs were not revolutionaries: "This isn't a put-down, but *revolutionaries do not make it in this system.*"[24] But that analysis seemed extreme to most, and a middle theoretical ground, therefore, emerged. As Edward Taub put it, "Businessmen can run rock through their $$$ channels, but none can control or regulate the beat, the intangibles which force a person closer to his or her body. Of course, rock n' roll won't make the revolution but be it ever so humble, it's playing its role."[25]

The Importance of the Lyrics

Although the hippies argued that rock was a totality and that its meaning was not mainly embodied in the words of its songs, it is obvious that rock lyrics inevitably had a great deal to do with the counterculture's values. They reflected those values, and in turn they helped shape them.

J. L. Simmons and Barry Winograd, in their 1966 survey of the emerging counterculture, detected two essential messages in contemporary rock lyrics: "Come swing with me," an exhortation to drop out of mainstream society (and not so subtly an invitation to have sex), and "Myself a stranger in a world I never made," an indictment of majority society and a declaration of alienation.[26] Those kinds of themes arose again and again. Rock lyrics sang the imminent demise of the dominant culture, the urgency of cultural revolution, the dead end of modern technological culture.

Some fairly specific analyses of the content of lyrics was undertaken in hippie days. The scholar James T. Carey undertook one of the more detailed studies, analyzing 176 songs (117 of them judged to be rock) popular during a three-month period in 1966. Carey determined that rock supported "new values" (i.e., countercultural values) in 68.1 percent of its lyrics, whereas other forms of music (blues, country, others) supported "old values" (i.e., mainstream values) at an even higher rate, sometimes over 80 percent of the time.[27] At their heart, Carey argued, rock lyrics urged listeners to maximize their freedom in interpersonal relationships and to drop out of conventional society.[28]

Much analysis was applied to the superstars, of course, and preeminently to Bob Dylan. One writer found the heart of Dylan to lie in analyzing America as a speed culture, in perceiving that "most of our technology and institutions are in effect artificial stimulants, which combine to keep us moving faster and faster." In a song like "Desolation Row," Dylan was warning us to stay away from mainstream society's dead end.[29] A bit more cosmically, Ralph J. Gleason summarized Dylan thus: "He is saying, in short, that the entire system of Western society, built upon Aristotelian logic, the Judeo-Christian ethic and upon a series of economic systems from Hobbes to Marx to Keynes, does not work."[30]

Dylan, though, was notoriously reticent about such analysis. A typical interview:

> Q: Your songs are supposed to have a subtle message.
> A: Subtle message?
> Q: Well, they're supposed to.
> A: Where'd you hear that?
> Q: In a movie magazine?
> A: Oh,—Oh God! Well, we won't—we don't discuss those things here.

* * *

> Q: Is there anything in addition to your songs that you want to say to people?
> A: Good Luck.
> Q: You don't say that in your songs.
> A: Oh, yes I do, every song tails off with "Good Luck,—I hope you make it."[31]

An interview with John Lennon was only slightly less cryptic:

> Q: What about philosophical analyses of your songs?
> A: . . . I write lyrics that you don't realize what they mean till after. ESPECIALLY some of the better songs or some of the more flowing ones, like "Walrus." The whole first verse was written without any knowledge. And "Tomorrow Never Knows"—I didn't know what I was saying, and you just find out later, that's why these people are good on them.
> Q: Pop analysts are often trying to read something into songs that isn't there.
> A: It is there. It's like abstract art really. It's just the same really. It's just that when you have to think about it to write it, it just means that you labored at it. But when you *say* it, man, you know you're saying it, it's a continuous flow.

Q: [*lines from "Penny Lane"*] A pretty nurse is selling poppies from a tray / And though she thinks she's in a play / She is anyway.

A: It's always been a bit of "She's in a play, she is anyway heh heh" because you're saying that again and again, it's a game, man, it's a game, but because you mean it, it's all right, it's ok.[32]

Finally, meaning came when the song interacted with the listener. "Lucy in the Sky with Diamonds" was one of the most celebrated acid songs ever, what with its titular acronym, but the Beatles consistently maintained that the acronym was purely accidental: "We didn't notice it said 'LSD' until somebody told us. Everybody interprets things in his own way."[33]

Rock Capitalism

Given the inescapable relation of rock to technology and therefore to money, capitalists popped up to profit from the sound. Most hippies resented rock capitalism, at least when it was undertaken by persons whose hearts were not hip. Commercialization of music did not originate in counterculture days, but it did represent a special problem for a movement not fond of capitalism and in any event devoted to seeking its meaning outside the courts of the Establishment. As Jon Landau observed in *Rolling Stone,* itself a piece of rock-based capitalism, "Rock, the music of the Sixties, was a music of spontaneity. . . . As that spontaneity and creativity have become more stylized and analyzed and structured, it has become easier for businessmen and behind-the-scenes manipulators to structure their approach to merchandising music."[34]

Capitalists ended up making more money from the music than hippie musicians did, and the most popular artists inevitably became capitalists. But it wasn't just a matter of having cynical materialists cash in on hip music. The financial structure of things affected the music itself, commercializing rock as it looked for "short-term profit and premature hardening of the categories," which was "in almost dialectical opposition to the leading principles of this cultural revolution," which stood for "communalism, participation, and, where possible, joy," as hip writer David Satterfield put it.[35] Thus was the dilemma posed, and the counterculture never solved it—indeed could not have solved it, given the hippies' disdain for analysis and planning. The music was too important to boycott. There were a few vague calls for communal alternatives to concerts and records but never any workable programs.[36]

Perhaps the closest thing to a hip type of rock capitalism was the bootleg record industry, which made unauthorized recordings of live concerts and distributed copies of illicitly acquired unreleased commercial tapes. But the bootleggers had bills to pay and thus became underground capitalists themselves. Moreover, their products tended to be expensive and of low quality. Ultimately, therefore, the music that was the language of a generation was to a fair degree controlled by the interests it was supposed to be overthrowing. Period.

Festivals and Concerts as Sacramental Assemblies

The great rock festivals and concerts were the definitive gatherings of the countercultural faithful. They were as important to the hip world as any pilgrimages, crusades, or revivals have ever been to their own constituencies. They helped shape rock and provided the best opportunities for massive indulgence in the sacraments: dope, nudity, sex, rock, community.

The lesser services were the ballroom concerts that occurred in cities everywhere. In the right setting, a concert could be an enormous turn-on: "Call it salvation through Hard Rock," one hipster wrote. "Through total sensory involvement, the mind is to be freed."[37] Indeed, so important did the ballroom concerts become that the names of the biggest halls took on a mythic aura: Fillmore, East and West; Winterland; the Avalon.

But the ultimate experience came at the great outdoor festivals, which ironically charted their own demise, since their immense size and freewheeling nature—laws can't be enforced when 100,000 criminals are present—led to enormous public resistance to their existence. The chemistry of the festivals was complex. Music was the main attraction, nominally, but the real point was the community offstage. There was a sense of cultural identity at the festivals that simply could not be found elsewhere. The individual faded, and the crowd became an organism, "something alive of itself."[38] There was nothing more entirely hip than the festivals.

The two giant festivals of 1969 displayed the full spectrum of the potential and problems of the genre. Woodstock, in August, drew unfavorable comments at first in the public press, since it happened in the rain and suffered major breakdowns of support facilities, but it was quickly mythologized by the counterculture as the epitome of joy and peace.[39] Woodstock was to the hippies all and everything: a cataclysm, a political event, a religious experience, a glimpse of communal solidarity, the pinnacle of passive consumerism, and the first free dope territory in America.[40] A few days after it was over one participant proclaimed that "the historians will have to reckon with it . . . these young revolutionaries are on their way . . . to slough away the life-style that isn't theirs . . . and find one that is."[41] Woodstock was "a confused, chaotic founding of something new, something our world must now find a way to deal with. The limits have changed now, they've been pushed out, the priorities have been re-arranged, and new, 'impractical' ideas must be taken seriously. The mind boggles."[42]

Woodstock was an obvious disaster: the sanitary, food, and medical facilities were overwhelmed and broke down while rain turned the meadow of farmer-host Max Yasgur into a quagmire. But all that simply made things cohere. "When a natural disaster strikes, people pull together in a rare way that they all remember with amazement years later," a Liberation News Service release announced a few days afterward.[43] Or, as Wavy Gravy (then known as Hugh Romney) said from the stage at the concert, "There's always a little bit of heaven in a disaster area." The physical conditions were bad, and Woodstock was after all a commercial enterprise operated for profit—but that didn't dampen the reality of the festival as a vision of a new reality. "Woodstock must always be [our] model of how good we will all feel after the revolution," Andrew Kopkind wrote, summing up the consensus.[44]

As it turned out, it was never quite to happen again. But the dream had been dreamed, and was not easily stilled: "Maybe, just maybe, it will be a new beginning for us despite our walking away from the most beautiful experience many ever had. . . . We now know we can live together as we had only done previously in our fantasies. No one will leave here the same person that existed before. For a few days we were all in a beautiful place. Can we do it again? All I know is I don't want to leave here. I feel like I've come home."[45]

If Woodstock was a glimpse of the best the future could hold, the Rolling Stones concert at the Altamont Raceway in the San Francisco Bay area a few weeks later provided a refresher course in grim reality. As the *Berkeley Barb* recorded it, "Someone was knifed to death. Lots of people were beaten. Love and peace were fucked by the Hells Angels in front of hundreds of thousands of people who did nothing. The brothers and sisters . . . could have cooled the Angels and any other violence spuming toughs, but they just let hate happen."[46]

What went wrong? Mismanagement, perhaps. Widespread rumor had it that the organizers of the concert had hired the Hells Angels motorcycle gang as security guards, paying the Angels in advance in beer.[47] Or perhaps heaven can be achieved only once. Whatever the case, soon after Woodstock peace and joy had given way to ugliness. Some went so far as to say that the concert marked the end of hip.[48] Few were as optimistic as Timothy Leary: "One thing that has to be said about Altamont is that there were three or four hundred thousand people there who did sit peaceably and get high and watch the sun and the clouds and the stars and listen to the music and were not at all involved in the violence. . . . There were less than fifty violent people there in a throng of 400,000. In a sense Altamont is a Microcosm of the overall political situation. 99% of everybody wants to get high, and groove and love."[49] Some could even dismiss the murder: "Four babies are born and four people die. An even exchange of souls."[50]

In any event, most remembered that the festivals on the whole were overwhelmingly positive events. Good reports continued to filter in from festivals in the years following Woodstock and Altamont. Thus festivals were mythologized as high-water marks of the counterculture, giving those attending—and even those just dreaming of attending—a taste of Nirvana.

Former residents of the Morning Star Ranch commune gath-
ered at the Human Be-In reunion in San Francisco in 2007.
Photo illustration by Ramón Sender.

From the Twin Oaks community you could go just about anywhere.
Photo by Timothy Miller.

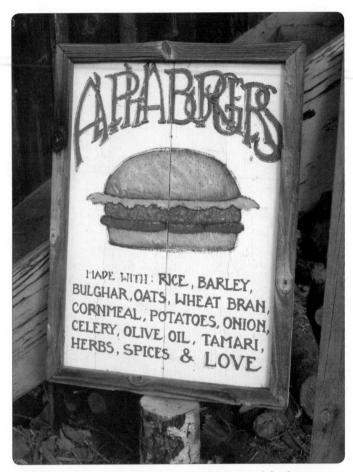

Counterculturists were at the forefront of the natural-foods movement. These Alphaburgers were created at Alpha Farm, Oregon, for use in the community's restaurant, Alpha Bits. Photo by Timothy Miller.

Anonymous cartoon.

American culture was at a dead end, the hippies argued. Copyright by R. Crumb, 1990. Used with permission of Last Gasp of San Francisco.

The New Left and the hippies were often at odds, but they had much in common. John Sinclair, manager of the rock group MC5, and his office illustrate the overlap. From the John and Leni Sinclair Collection, Michigan Historical Collection, Bentley Historical Library, University of Michigan.

There were relatively few African American hippies, but they were readily accepted by the white majority. From the John and Leni Sinclair Collection, Michigan Historical Collection, Bentley Historical Library, University of Michigan.

WANTED

Jesus Christ

WANTED FOR SEDITION, CRIMINAL
ANARCHY, VAGRANCY, AND CONSPIR-
ING TO OVERTHORW THE ESTABLISHED
GOVERNMENT.

Dresses Poorly. Said To Be A Carpenter
By Trade, Ill-nourished, Has Visionary
Ideas, Associates With Common Working
People, The Unemployed And Bums.

Alien—Believed to be a Jew

Alias— 'Prince of Peace' King of the Jews'
'Son of Man' Light of the World', etc., etc.

Professional Agitator

Red Beard, marks on Hands and Feet—
The Result of Injuries Inflicted By an
Angry Mob Led By Respectable Citizens
and Legal Authorities.

The hippies admired a radical Jesus but not the churches
that operated in his name.

What could be finer than a healthy stand of marijuana? From the John and Leni Sinclair Collection, Michigan Historical Collection, Bentley Historical Library, University of Michigan.

As faculty members at Harvard University, Ralph Metzner and Timothy Leary were early prophets of LSD. Later they took up residence at Millbrook, an estate owned by the wealthy family of some of their followers. From the *New York Daily News*.

What the country needed most was dope, the hippies believed. Copyright 1990 by R. Crumb. Used with permission of Last Gasp of San Francisco.

Beware! **Young and Old—People in All Walks of Life!**

This may be handed you

by the friendly stranger. It contains the Killer Drug "Marihuana"-- a powerful narcotic in which lurks

Murder! Insanity! Death!

WARNING!

Dope peddlers are shrewd! They may put some of this drug in the 🫖 or in the ᶜᵒᶜᵏᵗᵃⁱˡ or in the tobacco cigarette.

WRITE FOR DETAILED INFORMATION, ENCLOSING 12 CENTS IN POSTAGE — MAILING COST

Address: **THE INTER-STATE NARCOTIC ASSOCIATION**

Old anti-marijuana posters were reprinted and became popular satiric artifacts in hip culture. From the Kansas Collection, University of Kansas Libraries.

Body paint, beads, and advocacy of the use of LSD were all thoroughly hip.

...usicians were important participants in the dope subculture. From the John
...ni Sinclair Collection, Michigan Historical Collection, Bentley Historical
..., University of Michigan.

LSD was the answer to everything. From the Kansas Collection, University of Kansas
Libraries.

Many countercultural posters glorified LSD. From the Kansas Collection, University of Kansas Libraries.

Hippies believed marijuana to be much healthier than tobacco.

Two hippie buttons expressed rather con

Rock m
and Le
Librar

Militant feminism became increasingly prevalent late 1960s and early 1970s.

An early poster promoting a new San Francisco band called the Jefferson Airplane, here with their original female singer, Signe Anderson.

The Mothers of Invention was one of the more unorthodox hippie bands. From the Kansas Collection, University of Kansas Libraries.

Domes made of automobile tops dominated the architecture of Drop City, near Trinidad, Colorado. Photo from Gene and Jo Ann Bernofsky.

Drop City. Photo from Gene and Jo Ann Bernofsky.

Many hippies explored the life of the spirit. This meditating couple with their baby were at The Farm, an ongoing hippie commune in Tennessee. Photo by David Frohman.

Plenty International, a charity founded at The Farm community, undertakes development projects around the world. This soy demonstration took place in Lesotho. Photo provided by Plenty International, www.plenty.org.

Hippie politics emphasized love, not violence.

The hippie love of nature and desire for a cleaner environment led many to try to eat healthier food. From the John and Leni Sinclair Collection, Michigan Historical Collection, Bentley Historical Library, University of Michigan.

Rationality was disdained by the hippies. Copyright 1990 by R. Crumb. Used with permission of Last Gasp of San Francisco.

A few of the thousands of children born at The Farm. Photo by Albert Bates, copyright 1990 by The Second Foundation. Used by permission.

Stephen Gaskin, the spiritual teacher of The Farm community, conducted Sunday services for hundreds each week. Photo by David Frohman.

Stephen Gaskin has conducted thousands of marriages at The Farm, and years after The Farm was founded the tradition continues. Photo by Timothy Miller.

Hundreds of residents gather for Sunday morning meditation at The Farm community. Photo by David Frohman.

The Farm community's charity, Plenty International, has long taken urban children to the country during the summer. Photo by Anita Whipple, www.plenty.org.

Hippie architecture was highly original. This hand-built home is at the Libre community in Colorado. Photo by Timothy Miller.

A row of mailboxes met one arriving at Tolstoy Farm, an early countercultural commune in Washington State. Photo by Timothy Miller.

Chapter 4
The Ethics of Community

Now you see. This is it—you only have to come here to realize it. That's why we haven't been hassled. All the county officials and inspectors who come here realize that this is a better way of life than theirs. They know this is the answer just as you do.

—Olompali Ranch commune member,
Berkeley Barb, July 12–18, 1968

Intentional community is a vision that has a long and honorable history in human culture. The Buddhist *sangha,* or monastic community, is alive and well after some 2,500 years, making it surely the oldest human institution. The early Christians practiced community of goods. In America, the original Native American settlers lived in close communities, and some of the later settlers established utopian settlements as well—Shakers, Harmonists, and Hutterites, to name only three of thousands of communal movements and colonies. Thus the communes of the hippies represented an old ideal—but one presented in new garb.

The hippies, for their part, were not always students of communal history, and in any event many believed, as one of them put it, that "the hippie development is of a totally new order, wherein the past, in a sense, is irrelevant."[1] For one thing, most earlier communes were based on either religious or radical political and social convictions, and thus had clear ideological centers and strong senses of purpose. Many hip communes, on the other hand, tended toward free expression, hedonism, and anarchy, and they represented an attempt to live the hippie ethical ideals of liberated sex, use of dope, love, and sharing. Although the majority did not last more than a year or two, they attracted hundreds of thousands of residents and even more sympathetic visitors. And more than a few of them have survived, some having long since passed a quarter century of longevity, which makes them "successful" in Rosabeth Moss Kanter's widely cited analysis, and they represent tangible remaining links with hip culture.[2]

Several have tried to estimate the size of the hippie communal movement. Jules Siegel, writing in 1970, quoted a *Newsweek* estimate of 500 communes with 10,000 members in 1969, and a listing of 120 active communes in the *Modern Utopian*.[3] Benjamin Zablocki estimated in 1971 that there were then some 1,000 rural countercultural communes and about 200 urban communes.[4] Keith Melville, in 1972, similarly estimated the number of communes as "at least a thousand."[5] Judson Jerome, whose analysis probed more deeply than most, estimated that there were tens of thousands of communes with, altogether, perhaps 750,000 members.[6] And beyond those who actually lived in communes, thousands more who were, for whatever reason, unable to live in them admired the whole effort from afar. The ideal of community, in short, was powerful in the counterculture.

Communalism was present from the earliest days of the counterculture. Several communes founded in the 1950s and early 1960s (such as Tolstoy Farm in Washington State and Millbrook, the psychedelic commune of Timothy Leary and associates, both founded in 1963) showed early earmarks of a new, countercultural communal style, but the first commune that could be called full-blown hip was Drop City, founded in 1965 outside Trinidad, Colorado. Originally established as an artists' community, its striking domes covered with automobile tops became a prominent landmark in the hip communal scene, and it lasted through the heyday of the counterculture until its demise in 1973.[7] Another early entrant was the open-land Morning Star Ranch outside Occidental, California, founded in 1966. The mushrooming of communes after Morning Star, however, was widely believed in hippiedom to be related to the proliferation of rock festivals. The festivals were short-lived communes of a sort, as indeed were other music festivals before them. David Satterfield put it this way: "Communalism and participation, both, are best synthesized on a musical level in traditional festivals like the old-time fiddlers' conventions. But the interaction of different social classes is more advanced in Bluegrass festivals, where dancing gives way to actually picking music together."[8]

So the rock festivals took an existing phenomenon to a new level of intensity. Festival participants repeatedly emphasized an overwhelming sense of community that provided an impulse for continuing communal experimentation. The definitive festival in this regard was, of course, Woodstock, which was held in 1969. Reports on Woodstock in the underground press repeatedly stressed the feeling of unity: "Everyone needed other people's help, and everyone was ready to share what he had as many ways as it could be split up. Everyone could feel the good vibrations."[9] And from that feeling came the vision that free people could create "instant communities" where they could "live on their own terms."[10] The Hog Farm commune of New Mexico was influential at Woodstock. It was a working commune that provided support services (food, medicine, crisis intervention) as the festival's "Please Force." Although thousands of communes predated Woodstock, that festival became the symbol of a new cultural reality in which the call to community was compelling.

But rock did not contribute to communalism only at the point of the festival. The music itself was believed to feed the communal impulse: "the rock experience at its most intense is an imitation of engulfment and merger, a route to a flowing, ego-transcending oneness. As fans and enemies alike know, rock sound overwhelms separateness, the mental operations that discern and define here and there, me and not me. . . . Pounded by volume, riddled by light, the listener slides free from the restraining self and from the pretenses of a private 'unique' rationality."[11] Moreover, many rock bands themselves were models of communal living centered on a specific purpose.[12] One writer called them "super-families," "far more intimately interrelated and integrated than any corporate ensembles in the past"; indeed, rock itself was a "tribal phenomenon, immune to definition."[13] The band members were idealized as like unto the troubadours of old, singing and playing "to make people happy and to keep food in their mouths."[14]

So rock was seen as an essential in the rise of communalism. It helped people realize, as Tuli Kupferberg put it, that "two can live more better (as we used to say at P.S. 82) than one. So can three or four (or any number?)."[15] And the ultimate vision was one of cosmic-level communalism: "We are moving towards a conscious community of artists and lovers who live together, work together, share all things—smoke dope together, dance and fuck together, and spread the word together every way we can—through our dress, our freedom of movement, our music and dance, our economy, our human social forms, through our every breath on this planet."[16]

Dope, it should be noted, played its own role in the rise of communalism. Dope engendered a sort of community of its own in the sense that lawbreakers have something important in common, and that if they stick together they will probably improve their chances of staying out of jail. Rural communes might be isolated enough that the use of dope would be relatively difficult for the authorities to detect, and it is fair to surmise that the search for inconspicuous places to grow marijuana prompted more than one hippie to move to a rural commune.

Beyond that, dope was believed to spread the communal spirit. As Stanley Krippner and Don Fersh noted, dope tended "to weaken ego boundaries, leading an individual to conclude that 'we are all one.'"[17]

Community as an Ideal

Countercultural communes were means rather than ends. The end was affinity, communication, humans caring for each other, a new way of living. The communes were, in the words of one hip writer, "a means, a way, to bring us and our people closer together—closer to social freedom."[18] As another put it, "The commune itself is not an end product or a beginning. It's only an experience where we can learn to communicate in this way."[19] A hip observer identified only as Gorkin, writing for the *Village Voice* in 1969, had this to say:

> And then, suddenly it hits you like a ton of bricks. These hippies, these rebels, these dropouts, left to their own devices, what have they done? What new and dangerous things have they done? Why, they have fashioned a life composed of community, hard work, the family, religion. They have re-created (in their own image, to be sure) an old knowledge fired by a new passion, born of original discovery. They have given new life to old, old needs. Because what they want, in a word, is only a real life. Not a novel life. Not an aboriginal, orgiastic fantasy of a life. Only a *real* life.
>
> The urgency of this need, and only the urgency of this need, accounts for the continued existence of the communes.[20]

The new life being pursued by the communards was a deliberate repudiation of majority society. The communes were a major vehicle for dropping out of the old and into the new. As religious studies scholar William C. Shepherd observed, "in counter culture religiosity there is not so much a balanced dialectic between communitas and society, but instead an emphatic insistence that the communitas is the real thing, that one in fact need not reenter the ordinary world, that one can somehow abnegate its rules altogether not just momentarily."[21] That feeling of dropping out and building anew gave communes much of whatever strength they had. It provided a sort of emotional solidarity in a commune which, as Ed Schwartz put it, does not come from physical closeness itself, as any subway rider knows.[22]

The precise content of this solidarity defies exact definition, however. Robert Houriet, an early and perceptive observer of hip communes, asserted that it could not be understood with analytical tools, since the communes depended on a totally different consciousness than the straight world did, one that would not separate person and nature, self and society.[23] The trappings of communes, such as leftist ideology, communist economics, sexual freedom, and so forth, all faded before this fundamental consciousness. The goal was to become one in the New Age, to submerge the ego into the common mind and heart. Persons kept their distinctive abilities and needs, but the goal was to integrate those abilities and needs with the good of the community.

The Rural Impulse

The counterculture grew up largely in cities, and its participants came primarily from metropolitan areas, so it is of interest to note that hippie communes were ideally located in the country, even if real-world contingencies, such as proximity to jobs, forced a great many of them to be situated in towns and cities.[24] According to the counterculture, not only were cities physically intolerable for life ("Just name me one person who could live there without some kind of mind-fucking Forget pill ingested daily, or seven times daily, pills and smokes, tokes and needles, tabs and hits"),[25] they were also incompatible with a liberated or tribal lifestyle. The only places where urban hip living was possible, according to Raymond Mungo, were those in which the counterculture was so populous as to make good commercial sense to capitalists.[26] "Yes—brotherhood cannot develop inside the city. . . . Grab a car, some acid, (and of course man's staple—marijuana) and head for the ocean (or the woods, or actually anyway towards a decentralized humanoid existence)."[27] Those in cities became infected with classic rural romanticism: an "army of peaceful guerillas [is] ready to turn [its] back on the already ravaged cities and the inoperable 'life-styles,' imminently prepared to move onto the mist-covered fields and into the cool, still woods."[28] The appeal was powerful and mystical. Timothy Leary put it succinctly: "The key issue . . . is LAND."[29]

But a practical problem immediately presented itself: where does a group of voluntarily poor young persons find land to live on? Although several communes were fortunate enough to have wealthy patrons capable of paying for the real estate, buying land required more capital than was available to the

typical hippie, to say the least. Buying land, anyway, seemed a wrong beginning, as Raymond Mungo noted: "It is a foolish notion, this land ownership;
and men are made fools by it. . . . If you belong to the land, you'll stay there;
but if the land belongs to you, you'll lose it for sure, in some way."[30]

Some had visions of free land, opened to all comers by those fortunate
enough to be able to own it. The archetypal experiment of that type was conducted by the musician Lou Gottlieb, who opened his Morning Star Ranch
without restriction. Gottlieb idealistically claimed that his plan couldn't fail,
simply because the sort of person who would be attracted to such a concept
would be one with a high capacity for community and toleration of others. But
in practice Morning Star lurched between the Scylla of residents incapable of
the sharing and constructive giving necessary to make the community work,
and the Charybdis of continued confrontations with public officials determined to police such things as sanitation, minimum housing standards, and
illegal activity.[31]

Another solution to the problem of providing land for those who would
live on it was the proposed Earth People's Park. The idea took shape in the wake
of Woodstock; the original plan involved the purchase of a huge tract of land
(perhaps 5,000 acres or more, probably in New Mexico) with money raised
from a huge rock concert on the land itself.[32] Later a decentralized version of
the plan emerged, one which would have had many smaller parks. The Hog
Farm rolling commune eventually took over the project, raising seed money
for the plan, and in 1971 managed to purchase 592 acres of land in northern
Vermont near the Canadian border. Unfortunately, Earth People's Park attracted a "wedge of biker-junkies," as eminent Hog Farmer Wavy Gravy called
them, who drove out the more benign residents. Eventually the land was given
to the State of Vermont, which maintains it as part of Black Turn Brook State
Forest.[33]

The rural impulse was a part of the hippie preference for the natural over
the artificial, the organic over the plastic. In the country a clan could grow and
consume its own food free of contaminants, breathe clean air, be naked at will,
and be close to nature and to the cosmic forces. Getting clean and pure and
back to basics was a major part of the communal agenda.

New Family Structures

Part of the communal push was a new sense of family structure. For the hippies the biological family gave way to the cultural tribe. Kinship and relationships were up for grabs. Allen Ginsberg, for example, saw a host of new
possibilities: "We obviously are changing, altering in family structure. . . .

There's no reason to think it so strange that it might alter in a direction that some groups of people might want. And the tendency toward a commune and community and enlarged family is a very definite tendency. . . . I would see different kinds of family structure. Couple of girls with one guy, couple of guys with one girl, 20 girls, 20 guys, all making it if they want. Children held in common, matrilineal descent . . . sharing."[34] Timothy Leary identified the new family concept as making the difference between survival and failure of groups within the counterculture. Many "were not able to defend themselves because they didn't have any solid spiritual core, any rooted family centered-ness, he contended."[35] A new type of close-knit family was the goal, and communalism could help the hippies get there.

Varieties of Communes

The predominant public image of the hippie commune was of a rundown farm full of dirty druggies in some backwoods location, but in reality there was quite a diversity to the communal scene. There were urban and rural, drug-using and drug-free, egalitarian and chauvinistic, structured and anarchical, religious and secular communes, to name just a few of the antitypes.

Several hip authors constructed typologies of communes. Ed Schwartz, for example, categorized them by purpose and came up with four types:

1) Therapeutic communes were those formed for the working out of the common psychological problems or social situations of the persons involved, as in the case of women wrestling with sexism or young runaways trying to cope with their problems.

2) Fraternal communes were made up of lonely individuals who simply wanted to live with others.

3) Utopian communes were formed to demonstrate to the world a new way of living, to prove the superiority of the hip way of life. These groups were probably the ones which received the most public attention, but were not necessarily the most common.

4) Organizing communes were those with a common ideology, program, or strategy for social change; such communes were united largely by their participants' opposition to the war in Vietnam and, more broadly, to the prevailing sociopolitical system, their members sharing the risks of radical dissent.[36]

Schwartz missed one important countercultural communal type: the religious. New religions were part of the countercultural matrix, and several of them operated communes for some or all of their members. The Hare Krishna movement, founded in the United States in 1965 and intimately related to the hippies in its early years, was largely communal. The Jesus freaks who appeared in the latter days of hip founded an extensive network of communes. And independent spiritual communes were also founded in considerable numbers. The Farm in Tennessee, led by hip spiritual teacher Stephen Gaskin, had some 1,500 members at its peak and has continued on a smaller scale ever since.[37]

Many of the religious communes were not exactly fully countercultural, however, even though they drew their members from the ranks of the hippies, used the hip argot, and shared with the hippies an antiestablishment outlook. The Hare Krishnas, for example, rejected all intoxicants, nearly all sex, rock and roll and other Western music, and all kinds of activities not deemed properly transcendental. But boundary lines between hip and straight were always impossible to draw precisely, and the religious communes had feet in more than one world.

Another typology of communes was based upon the structures and organizational patterns that the groups took. One such scheme was proposed by Stanley Krippner and Don Fersh on the basis of their observation of eighteen substantial communes. They ended up with three types of communities: "The secular commune which is relatively unstructured and which functions with a minimum of administration" (the freewheeling Morning Star in California would again be a good example of that type); "the secular commune which is relatively structured and which operates within an administrative framework," one which often functioned because of the presence of a strong leader; and "the structured, highly-organized religious commune," such as New Vrindaban, the Hare Krishna communal farm in West Virginia, or the less sectarian but still spiritually oriented Lama Foundation at San Cristobal, New Mexico.[38] Many other typologies of communes could be constructed, but in the hip world categories were hardly rigid. Communalism in the counterculture was ideologically, organizationally, and spiritually diverse.

On the other hand, a few themes were widespread among the communes. Most of them professed to reject materialism in favor of spiritual and personal growth, however defined. They were usually committed to toleration, attracting and coping fairly well with a wide variety of members. They were bastions of the culture of opposition. By definition the communards were committed to dropping out of majority society. Finally, many commune residents tended to be inwardly oriented, wanting to live freely without interfering with or being interfered with by the outside world any more than was necessary.

The Downside

As beatific as the communal vision was, reality was something else. No hip commune avoided a host of problems, and in many cases the problems rose up to drown the commune. There are no reliable statistics here, but average longevity of the communes could not have been high.

One common problem in communes was that these "liberated" utopias all too often were not very enlightened about women's roles. Many hip women found communal life oppressive, and more than a few were led to the then-emerging women's movement both by their treatment at the hands of certain communal men and by the feminist solidarity that often developed among women at a commune. Kit Leder, reflecting on life in a twelve-member farm commune in the summer of 1969, wrote afterward,

> Even though there was no society-dictated division of labor, even though we had complete freedom to determine the division of labor for ourselves, a well-known pattern emerged immediately. Women did most of the cooking, all of the cleaning up, and, of course, the washing. They also worked in the fields all day—so that after the farm work was finished, the men could be found sitting around talking and taking naps while the women prepared supper. In addition to that, one of the women remained in camp every day in order to cook lunch—it was always a woman who did this, never a man. Of course, the women were excused from some of the tasks; for example, none of us ever drove a tractor. That was considered too complicated for a woman.[39]

Building on that analysis, Vivian Estellachild wrote of her experience living in two communes:

> Although communal living appears to be a step in the right direction, the hip commune uses women in a group way the same as the fathers did in a one-to-one way. The communes are too fluid to create any security for a woman. Her stability lost and isolation complete, she cannot be an effective force for change.
>
> The source of our oppression is *all men,* no exceptions for bells and beads.[40]

But it needs to be said as well that not all communes were oppressive. About the same time that Leder and Estellachild were finding communal life a dead end for women, Marilyn Foster was having an opposite experience in a Baltimore commune: "The men and women in Toad Hall have enabled each other to move outside of male-female roles and expectations. . . . Our community arrangement offers the support and acceptance necessary in a society which alienates us from who we are and where we want to go. We don't have all the answers—but we are picking up some good leads."[41]

Women's issues were not the only problems with communes. Ed Schwartz, in his discussion of communal problems, concluded that three general situations led to the communes' typically abbreviated longevity: members joined for very different personal reasons and thus the group lacked coherent direction; many communes failed to enforce agreements or rules, since an authoritarian structure tended to be suspect in the counterculture; and many communes were incapable of changing communal goals in response to new situations and insights. The fundamental problem, as Schwartz put it, was that for most people God was dead, and therefore there was no belief or ideology strong enough to sustain any but the most intensely religious communes.[42]

Certainly a major underlying source of communal problems was the fact that in many cases communes proved attractive to individuals whose interest in new ways of living was related to their failure to function effectively in conventional society—that is, persons whose basic nature or personal problems made them terrible candidates for group living. Horace Greeley—himself a vocal supporter of communalism in the nineteenth century—had identified that problem nearly a century before the hippies came along:

> A serious obstacle to the success of any socialistic experiment must always be confronted. I allude to the kind of persons who are naturally attracted to it. Along with many noble and lofty souls, whose impulses are purely philanthropic, and who are willing to labor and suffer reproach for any cause that promises to benefit mankind, there throng scores of whom the world is quite worthy—the conceited, played-out, the idle, and the good-for-nothing generally; who, finding themselves utterly out of place and at a discount in the world as it is, rashly conclude that they are exactly fitted for the world as it ought to be.[43]

So in reality many of the communes attracted more than their share of deadbeats, drunks, drug (as opposed to dope) users, abusers of women, and other undesirables. Communities with open-door policies—initially there were many of them—naturally suffered more from the problem than the more selective ones did. In any event, personnel problems had more than a little to do with the fact that most communes, and especially the anarchistic ones, were often short-lived. That said, hundreds of 1960s-era communes survived, and many of them are healthier than ever.

Whatever the stories of the triumphs and tragedies of specific communes, the counterculture retained its dedication to the ideal of community. Though some communes did not last long, the general consensus was that, as California counterculturist Gene Carlson put it, "all of the communities were successful for what was learned in them."[44] Ed Schwartz again: "Community is neither more nor less than a mutual commitment to share in the pursuit of a common vision; and given the conditions of the day, one would hope that it be the vision of justice for all. If the communes can generate this vision, if they can nurture and sustain it, then all power to them. If not, then all the power in the world will not rescue them from the morass in which they currently find themselves."[45]

A Note on Individualism and Collectivism

On several occasions observers of the counterculture criticized the hippies for being conformists in a movement that supposedly rejected conformism, for being obedient sheep instead of the individualists they claimed to be. Wrote one doctor sympathetic to the counterculture, "I'm concerned with the great deal of group conformity that exists in the hip movement. It's supposed to be the antithesis of conformity."[46] Others noted a paradox in the counterculture's embracing of communes along with anarchy and free self-expression.[47] For the hippies themselves, that criticism was misdirected. The world of hip never idealized individualism. After all, "individualism" of a particularly constrained type (the type more accurately labeled "selfishness") was one of the central cancers of Establishment society. It led people to be indifferent or antagonistic toward others; it moved people toward unconcern about the environment; it made social problems fester. Although the hippies were colorful, even flamboyant, in their rejection of majority society, individualism was not any kind of ultimate concern for them. As a hip writer wrote in an Atlanta underground paper, "Instead of millions of young individuals, what we now have is an entire generation moving headlong into a collective consciousness."[48]

Criticism of American individualism was, in fact, a staple topic for hip-oriented writers. "Individualism," wrote Philip Slater, "is a kind of desperate plea to save all mutants, on the grounds that we do not know what we are or what we need." Loss of individualism "in some degree, is just the price we must pay for a tolerable life in a tolerable community."[49] To the counterculture, the fruits of individualism were privatism, competition, elitism, selfishness, jealousy, and reinforcement of the territorial imperative, all of which were evil. "Generally we were raised in a world where survival was strictly for self, for self gain, for self survival. . . . Now the pendulum is coming to a point where the only way we will survive is when everybody is doing for each other," Gene Carlson observed.[50]

Slater described this excessive individualism as being uniquely related to American culture. America, he wrote, provides one of the few societies in which the welfare of the individual has not been subordinated to that of the group. "Americans are forced into making more choices per day, with fewer givens, more ambiguous criteria, less environmental stability, and less social structural support, than any people in history." Thus it is that the three "human desires" of community, engagement, and dependence have been "deeply and uniquely frustrated by American culture."[51]

Therefore the counterculture opted for collectivism. In the realms of both possessions and the self, self-denial for the community was the order of the day. At Woodstock, "although local residents were reported to be demanding 25 cents for a glass of water and $1 for a loaf of bread and a quart of milk, on the festival grounds, sharing what you had—whether a bonfire, an apple or a joint—was the order of the night."[52] Throughout the counterculture, the price of admission was "the sacrifice of one's individual pride, no one can do it by themselves, that's the trip back into the dark ages."[53] One learned "that one restricts one's freedom in order to taste the sweetness of freedom earned, freedom defined, freedom marked off; that one gains the whole of oneself by giving up a part of oneself; that [people], in order to call themselves anything, must call themselves members of a nation."[54]

So far from individualism was the counterculture that the exercise of the ego itself was regarded as needing tight limits. Raymond Mungo wrote that countercultural life required "a death of the ego."[55] Paul Goodman wrote that the original sin was to be on an ego trip that isolated one from the community.[56] In the place of individuals, the community itself became the basic reality.

Certainly the retreat from individualism was, as so many other things in the counterculture were, related to dope. Psychedelic experience was not just something that was internal and private for the individual; it was an article of faith that the expansion of mind helped one forego the ego and learn that there was, in Timothy Leary's expression, "one transient energy process hooked with the energy dance about him."[57]

And once the collective consciousness had been realized on that level, the way was opened for an individualism of sorts that was far better than the law of the jungle. It was an individualism that did not reduce self to selfishness, one which let each person have a sphere of operation within the community, one which allowed for an innocent, free flowering of personality that was compatible with the needs of the people united. It is in that spirit that the countercultural aphorism "Do your own thing" should be understood. Flamboyant self-expression was wonderful—but one's first commitment had to be to the group, not the self.

Chapter 5

Forward on All Fronts: The Ethics of Cultural Opposition

REMEMBER: The *first* revolution (but not of course the last) is in yr own head. Dump out *their* irrational goals, desires, morality.

—Tuli Kupferberg, in Joseph Berke, *Counter Culture* (1969)

The idea is that we have no ideas. We want to abolish ideas. What we want is peace, communication, and escape from automation.

—"Anthony," *Florida Free Press,* June 30, 1968

The counterculture never saw itself as just another subculture. It was the Disloyal Opposition to Establishment culture. And from the beginning cultural conflict was the order of the day, if only, as the hippies saw it, because the majoritarians insisted on confrontation with the hippies, as in arresting them for sale and possession of dope and trying to block rock festivals and communes. Thus the culture of peace and love was also a culture of confrontation and conflict.

The major themes examined so far—dope/drugs, sex, rock and roll, and community—were hardly the only categories of the new cultural ethics. The optimistic hippies had a vision of creating a whole new culture, and the new ethics they proposed touched nearly all parts of life. This chapter provides an overview of several other important themes in hip ethics, demonstrating the breadth of the hippie critique and the depth of the discontent and alienation the hippies felt from the dominant culture.

One need not read very far in countercultural literature to realize the centrality of its contention that American culture had, by the mid-twentieth century, reached a dead end. The stranglehold of technocrats, bigots, and incompetents on American institutions had reached the point, the hippies believed, that an even moderately sensitive person had to cry Enough! There has to be something better than all of this!

Cultural opposition was not, however, merely a nay-saying. Although hipness was a rebellion, it was a rebellion with a vision, a sort of insurrectionary artist's eye. The hippies offered broad goals for a humane society: creativity, decentralization, distrust of bureaucratic and hierarchical structures, freedom, pleasure, antiauthoritarianism, direct and honest contact among persons, and the discarding of restrictions and inhibitions. Examining such themes is the job of this chapter.

Love Is All You Need

Nothing more identified the counterculture in its early days than "peace and love." The hippies were the love generation, a people of peace, sweetness, flowers, light, optimism. The epitome of the spirit of love came with the great Be-Ins (unstructured massive gatherings of the countercultural faithful), the first of which was at Golden Gate Park in San Francisco on January 14, 1967, at which it was reported that there was "no anger, no reproach for the act of non-love. . . . Some say as many as [20,000] were present and all seemed filled, contented and giving."[1] Love was one of the most frequently used words in the hippie vocabulary, and even the editors of *Time* concluded in their 1967 cover story on the hippies that "the key ethical element in the hippie movement is love—indiscriminate and all-embracing, fluid and changeable, directed at friend and foe alike."[2]

"Love" is a word with a variety of definitions, and it meant several things to the counterculture. In its most simple and direct sense, love was an emotion, a state of mind, a feeling that radiated optimistic moral power. Hippies sometimes quoted parts of the classic poem on love, the thirteenth chapter of Paul's first letter to the Corinthians, concluding, as one put it, that "Paul's statement is comprehensive and goes further than anything to be heard so far in the debate on love."[3] It was a love that transcended all human divisions, or should: "Love the people you hate, for you should pity them—the cop who's full of animal fear. . . . Love the tortured souls who have all the material things, but nothing spiritual to make their lives bearable."[4]

This freely giving love was essentially a state of mind, but it was held to issue in ethical conviction, and thus love could become action: "It can change and create. It can move and it can shake moral, political, ethical, economic, and spiritual consciousness."[5] Applied love resulted in the practice of the Golden Rule and in concern for all beings. "We can do it, but it has to be 'WE'!!!!!! . . . all these lonely people need only someone to give a shit about them."[6] And this love was not merely a matter of creating some passing bit of goodness for a moment. If truly practiced, it would reform the world. It would counter the existing way of hate, epitomized by the politics of capitalists and communists alike, the politics of exploitation and war that had led the world to the brink of catastrophe.[7] Indeed, hippies argued, love was the *only* answer to the overwhelming problems afflicting the world. Applied love was the only way to human community, to a real solution of the world's seemingly intractable ills.

For most hippies, love meant nonviolence. Violence, they argued, was the product of a corrupt society and was one of that society's dead ends. "Violence is a means to itself only, ain't nothing good gonna come of it never. Never has, never will," went a typical hip pronouncement.[8] Thus the love ethic could be a bridge between the cultural hippies and the New Left politicos—the main agenda item of the New Left was, after all, ending the war in Vietnam, and what higher expression of love could there be than peace?

Love in practice could be organized. The Diggers, who surfaced in San Francisco and elsewhere, and other similar groups were prime models of organized love.[9] In an early statement, the Diggers announced that they were trying "to help motivate the youth who move about without direction, to discover the rich creative potential inherent in them and to establish positive goal-directed activities for themselves." To that end they supplied "food and housing for those in need, not to create dependency, but as a starting point towards self-realization and independence," on the theory that the solution of individual problems pointed the way to the building of "the creative society we all desire."[10] They gave the public free food, ran free stores, and provided free places to sleep. They even undertook the huge task of feeding the thousands of people at the Be-Ins: "In the spirit of the Five Thousand, the Diggers began to feed the multitude," one hip reporter wrote concerning the first big Be-In.[11] Other groups did work along the same lines, among them the Provos of Berkeley and the Church of Holy Water.[12]

But the hippies hardly achieved perfect love. They were human, after all, and therefore flawed. The more perceptive among them tempered idealism with realism. One wrote, "Perhaps we're no different from our parents after all. We're just stoned when we inflict pain upon our brothers."[13] Another speculated, "I think we have fallen prey to the sickness which we fight. We have begun to hate those who do not love and by so doing we have become those we fight against. . . . I say we need a true revolution. A revolution of non-violence and love."[14]

Many who seized the rhetoric of peace and love quickly perverted it. Protesting that perversion was the point of the funeral that marked the "Death of Hip" in San Francisco in the fall of 1967: the wave of love, or love-talk, was being usurped by many who did not know its spirit.[15] Sometimes the degradation of love was commercial, as when in the Haight-Ashbury an old greasy spoon became the "Love Cafe," serving "love burgers" and "love dogs," or when advertisers put together a "Love Guide," a map of Haight-Ashbury businesses. In another case, the "Love Conspiracy Commune" put on a "Love Circus" at $3.50 per head. It was picketed by Diggers and others who claimed that it was an "exploitation of love"—"if it's really love it would be free."[16] "There's nothing like a little love, and most Haight-Ashbury merchants are shucking it out by the truckload," wrote one counterculturist before the Summer of Love had even begun.[17]

Given the problems with the noble idea of love, perhaps it is not too surprising that some counterculturists found the entire idea hopeless. A few, at least, came to believe that love simply was not realistic in a world of militarism and hatred: "Tuning in to the flowers and to love and turning on to acid is very nice, but it's schizophrenia just like the suburban kind."[18]

The majority, however, were profoundly dedicated to peace and love. Love, after all, was all you needed.

Political Ethics

Many of the most heartfelt hippies were decidedly cultural, not political, in their outlook, and they often chastised the New Left for its rather puritanical devotion to social change through political action. But the hippie lifestyle had political implications. Persons living on the boundary of what was socially acceptable could not always avoid political reality, no matter what they thought of it.

Certainly the hippies had no single approach to politics. Two schools of thought dominated the fragmented field. One of those schools was that of disinvolvement, of dropping out of society, of refusing to participate in anything that smacked of politics, of avoiding dealing with the prevailing powers if at all possible.[19] The other was that of cultural revolution, of fighting in the social and political arena for reform of laws and mores that obstructed countercultural activities and occasionally for other humanitarian political ends, such as curbing private property rights. Relatively few hippies seemed to cling consistently to either of the two camps. Even such a prominent figure as Raymond Mungo, who, after his disavowal of activism, was virulently antipolitical, found it necessary to engage in a politics of confrontation when he refused military induction. Despite his skepticism that radical activity in any case would ever make any difference, he noted that "I've always been absolutely sure that every man who refuses induction is one less man in the Army, one more on the positive side of the chalk line."[20]

On the whole, disengagement was at least theoretically the more attractive pole for the counterculture. Two main arguments were advanced for that position. First, there was the cynical conviction that however right a political opinion might be, there was no use in trying to effect change because it simply wouldn't work. As Mungo, the archetypal theoretician of cynicism, put it, "I am sufficiently tuned-in to the century to realize that we men never really get *anywhere*. It's always more of the same, so to speak—birth, life, death. . . . We do tend to end up where we started."[21]

Some counterculturists had spent many years battling for civil rights, working to end the war in Southeast Asia, trying to reorder national economic priorities, attempting to reform the schools, and so forth, and they did not see any significant results for their considerable effort. Further, they believed that any short-term gains were offset by a lack of long-term improvement.[22] In such circumstances, it was not difficult to sink into cynicism. Hippies with political experience had the feeling that they knew that of which they spoke, and that they therefore had a finer insight on politics than did revolutionaries who had not yet seen the total uselessness of demonstrations and other political activities.[23] Even such a simple act as voting was often condemned as useless, or worse. "Voting is an illusory act. . . . Not once has a 'leader' been truthful to his 'people.' . . . Don't vote."[24]

Beyond cynicism, some argued that politics was simply not of concern to free people. Cultural revolution did not involve political activity so much as it did simply being liberated. One "characteristic of the new revolutionist," a hippie wrote, "is that he is not content to wait for the revolution, is in his life style anticipating the revolution, is in a sense living the revolution."[25] Another concurred, "The age of politics is finished. . . . The only way you get freedom is by deciding that you're free. If you fight authority, you acknowledge it, you give it power. If authority is ignored, it doesn't exist any more."[26] To those who complained that change requires a political program, the counterculture replied, in the words of Ralph Gleason and Raymond Mungo,

No, the hippies and the Beatles and the Pop musicians present no Program for Improvement of the Society. What they do is to present a program for improvement of the young people of the world. You can't change the society until you reach a state of grace.[27]

I no longer have any kind of program to save the world, let alone nineteenth-century Marxism, except perhaps to pay attention to trees. . . . I'll just go my solitary way and strive to enjoy what may well be the last days of this beautiful but deteriorating planet.[28]

Politics held no salvation for anyone. Hope came only in life, in the lives of individuals and in freedom itself. "Power to no one. Life to everyone."[29]

Some writers saw dope as pointing the way to political disinvolvement. Dope was held to communicate to the user that "you don't overcome a negative force by opposing it directly on the level of force itself."[30] Beyond that, psychedelics were held to lead the user to a new way of life lacking the leadership-oriented organization that is essential to conventional politics.

Nature and the Environment

The counterculture harbored many early and articulate critics of the increasingly obvious and severe degradation of the environment that was clearly accelerating in the mid-1960s. Most popular hippie writings on the environment tended to be antitechnological and philosophically based on Eastern metaphysics and pieces of the Native American tradition. The basic proposition was simple: human beings were an integral part of nature, not its masters, and one was thus obligated to adapt oneself to the flow of things instead of interfering with it and trying to conquer it, which was perceived to be the traditional Western way of dealing with nature. A fairly typical sentiment came from the Beatle George Harrison: "The more you meditate and the more you harmonize with life in general then the more nature supports you."[31]

A 1967 list of "Ten commandments for getting to the city of God" published in the San Francisco Oracle included "revere nature."[32] That could mean many things, including environmental activism, outdoor living, and opposition to experimentation on animals, among others.[33] Similarly Charles Reich, presenting a bill of seven particulars summarizing the nature of the American crisis to which he saw the hippies as responding, included in his list "uncontrolled technology and the destruction of the environment."[34] But the bottom line for the counterculture was learning the ancient truth that the human race is finally only one tiny part of great nature, and that the race's survival depends on learning to live harmoniously with nature, not on conquering it or beating it back.

In the early days of the counterculture, in the middle 1960s, the perception that the earth itself was gravely endangered was still a bit of a novelty, not widely held as it is today. It was here, perhaps better than in any other place, that the ethics of the counterculture was visionary. Many derided hippies in the 1960s for their rather naive love of nature and sense of portending doom. Half a century later they don't look quite so silly.

Dropping Out

Closely related to the countercultural view of politics was the admonition (popularized as a slogan by Timothy Leary) to drop out, to quit Establishment society and drop into the new age. It was a concept sufficiently important to the counterculture that sociologist and psychotherapist Lewis Yablonsky included it as one of the ten points of his "Psychedelic Creed."[35]

Dropping out was to some extent political ("We are absolved from all Allegiance to the United States Government and all governments controlled by the menopausal," Leary wrote), but it was broader than just that. It was the disowning of a life oriented toward work, status, and power. It was a search for poverty, simplicity, and new ideas.[36] Richard Alpert (later Baba Ram Dass) called it a reorganization of personal relations so as to make each moment meaningful.[37]

In some cases, dropping out was associated with the individualized search for truth and enlightenment that characterizes the lives of most of the great religious figures:

> A drop-out is a retrogression; the psychologists call it "positive disintegration." You drop out of the ego-addicting symbol attachment into the billion year old flow of electrical energy. You relinquish the I, Me and Mine of existence and expand into the selfless void of essence, not Mine, but thine. That is the message of all the great masters.
>
> Each man is his own Buddha, on his own trip. Find your own way of dropping out. . . . Remember, everything is progress.[38]

The phenomenon of voluntary detachment from majority society had good historical precedent. In response to those Christians and Jews who denounced the ethic of dropping out, hippies noted that the observance of a Sabbath, "at least theoretically, is simply a weekly 'dropping out' from everyday activity for the purpose of reflection and spiritual renewal."[39]

Dropping out was more a concept than a program, for although a few hippies had independent means, most had to make a living. Only a few could be supported directly by hip culture—the dope dealers, a few of the musicians and artists, some merchants. So if only for economic reasons, most kept one foot firmly in Establishment society. Nevertheless, the sense of psychic separation from the mainstream was important. One knew that one was free, and, within the limits of the mundane needs of life, lived that way.

Money and Materialism

The Woodstock festival of 1969, as planned and temporary as it was, was ever afterward idealized by hippies as a time and place "free from the need of money,"[40] and thus a model for life in the new age. Counterculturists examined the money-based economic systems of the world and found them wanting. Lawrence Lipton wrote in 1970, "Moneytheism is a religion. It began as a religion and to this day it has all the mythology and ritual that goes with religion."[41]

The hippies proclaimed what in a sense is obvious but few admit: money itself is meaningless. It is, in the words of Alan Watts, so many poker chips, without intrinsic value and (Watts argued) outdated in an electronic age.[42] The problem, as Watts expressed the ethic that the hippies embraced, is that most people confuse the artificial construct that is money with wealth, which is "the sum of energy, technical intelligence and raw materials."[43]

The counterculture proved the depth of the entrenchment of that confusion on several occasions. On the best publicized of them, Abbie Hoffman, Jerry Rubin, and several others demonstrated their disdain for money by throwing thirty or forty dollar bills (they claimed it was a thousand) from the visitors' gallery onto the floor of the New York Stock Exchange with the declaration, "Money is over."[44] The Exchange was sufficiently horrified to install a pane of glass at the front of the gallery to prevent any recurrence of the outrage. Other similar acts elsewhere met with similar responses. The American public was clearly not ready to follow Rubin's suggestion to "use your money as toilet paper."[45]

Yet the counterculture was not entirely—or even mainly—free from the lure of the allegedly evil artificial substance. Stewart Brand provided a clever case in point when, at the June 1971 party to celebrate the demise of the original Whole Earth Catalog series, he tried to give the 1,500 assembled people $20,000 on the sole condition that they come to some agreement as to its use. Some wanted to divide it on the spot; others came up with a range of proposals, none of which met with general acceptance. Finally, the surviving $14,905 (the balance had already disappeared into the crowd) was entrusted to the one individual present who "seemed to hate money the most." The last report, months later, was that the individuals involved had a tentative plan to establish a "synergy warehouse" to "create an alternative urban environment," but the specifics were still lacking and nothing concrete had been done.[46] Brand had made his point well, that the anti-money counterculture was still very uptight about it all.

The hippies lived in the real world, but their ideal remained a disavowal of the materialism of American society. At the very least, they proclaimed a disavowal of consumer culture, believing, as Raymond Mungo wrote, that "a man with good boots on his feet and 9 dollars in his pocket can get most anything he needs in this world."[47] Money symbolized many evils. The materialism and greed that characterized America needed to give way to a new order "free from property hang-ups, free from success fixations, free from positions, titles, names, hierarchies, responsibilities, schedules, rules, routines, regular habits."[48] As social psychologist and educator Kenneth Keniston said, the counterculture sought "new *values for living*, values that will fill the spiritual emptiness created by material affluence."[49] Mungo: "We never ask each other 'what do you *do*?' in the sense of 'how do you make money?' Many of us make no money at all, others do but it is something less than incidental to our lives, which are really about a million forces having nothing to do with career, profession, or money."[50]

Again, however, all this is either blue-sky romanticism or evidence of social privilege. Some of the hippies who talked the most about abolition of money were children of privilege for whom the grinding reality of real want was nonexistent. The poor rarely found their young turning into hippies.

Work and Play

In a nation built on the Protestant ethic, the counterculture proclaimed the heresy that play was better than work. Play has, in fact, been held to be a central concept of the counterculture: as one hip theoretician put it, "There is one quality which enlivens both the political and cultural denominations of Youth protest; which provides its most important innovations; which has the greatest relevance for the future; which is the funniest, freakiest and the most effective. This is the element of play."[51]

Johan Huizinga, in his classic study of play, found freedom to be its major characteristic.[52] For the counterculture, freedom was important, but so was fun. Play "adorns life, amplifies it and is to that extent a necessity both for the individual—as a life function—and for society . . . as a cultural function."[53]

The counterculture differentiated play from organized athletics, which it saw as a "ritualized, legitimised aggression narcotic; hard work, competitive, corrupt."[54] The perfect countercultural game/sport was Frisbee, with no score-keeping, no competition, no rules, and no apparent potential as a profitable spectator sport. (Those who eventually tried to make it a competitive sport thus profaned its essence.)

Play was seen as the wave of the future in that it offered a real alternative to the organization and regimentation that afflicted society. Those who failed to incorporate an element of play into their lives were missing out. Ron Jarvis wrote in a Houston underground paper, "One of the healthiest aspects, if not the core, of the young's defiance is its acceptance or its welcoming of pleasure and sensuality. No longer is it necessary for a revolutionary to be dour and severe. This outlook is what indicates the eventual success of our revolution over those of other times. No more guilt, no hideous neuroses or psychoses. Life is to be lived, not endured."[55] Allen Ginsberg agreed: "Life should be ecstasy. We need life styles of ecstasy and social forms appropriate to whatever ecstasy is available for whoever wants it."[56]

The work ethic was distinctly distasteful to the hippies, and it was bashed head-on, as by Abbie Hoffman:

> Take W-O-R-K. When we say that nobody is going to work in the new world, it really spooks them. Not ideology nor drugs. W-O-R-K. When you tell the straight world you are never going to work again they go into ulcers.
>
> I think this is because W-O-R-K is directly linked to the Judeo-Christian guilt complex. The original sin. W-O-R-K supposedly atones for all sins. The Protestant ethic has worked hand-in-hand with capitalism to keep the wheels rolling and the poor fuckers down in the mines.[57]

All of that does not mean that counterculturists were determined to never lift a finger again. What it did mean was that they were determined to avoid the slavery of drudgery, to change the situation in which, as Philip Slater wrote, "Technology makes core policy . . . and the humans adjust as best they can."[58] Charles Reich wrote that the counterculture was not opposed to work itself, but only to meaningless work, and that hippies worked as hard as anyone else at something they enjoyed doing—building a commune, constructing a people's park, pursuing a hobby.[59] Work directly related to pleasure and human needs became "work transformed," work that was fun to do.[60] As Tuli Kupferberg wrote, "Believe me when I say: if you enjoy it, it can still be good; it can still be 'work' (only we'll call it 'play'). Play is as good as work. Work has been defined as something you *dislike* doing. Fuck that. Do the Beatles *work?* Who cares. We like what they do."[61]

A fundamental reason why the counterculture could reject work was that work seemed to be moving toward obsolescence. The counterculture had a sense that modern technology was producing a cornucopia of goods and therefore that work, all the time, was no longer required of every member of society in order to supply the necessities of life. "The core of the old culture is scarcity," wrote Philip Slater, but scarcity no longer existed.[62] Without saying that scarcity could never come again, the hippies argued that at least in their time and place net scarcity existed only when it was artificially induced. Many existing jobs, they believed, were holdovers from the age of scarcity and thus totally useless. Eliminate the guards, customs agents, locksmiths, tax agents, salespersons, accountants, insurance agents, advertising agents, ticket agents, bankers, and all others whose jobs stem from scarcity, and a great deal of pointless human effort would be eliminated. And there was no need to worry about incentives, the hippies naively maintained; only a minority of the present workforce would need to labor if all the useless jobs were eliminated. There would, in short, be plenty for all with minimal effort.[63]

One of the chief countercultural complaints against automation and cybernation was that those forces had dehumanized society by making people slaves to machines. The post-scarcity point of view rehumanized technology without dismantling it. Kenneth Westhues argued that "the significance of the counterculture today is that it urges a break with the theory of rationalization in favor of the exciting possibilities a world created by rational thought permits."[64] And so in the counterculture, because "automation has replaced work, play assumes its rightfully central role."[65]

Ripping Off the Establishment

Most ethical systems include a fairly straightforward prohibition of theft. In general, the counterethics included such a prohibition, but in a few instances a case was made for a Robin Hood approach to stealing: there could be a moral justification for stealing from the rich.

In general, stealing was justifiable in the counterculture only if it was at the expense of those who were perceived to have stolen—legally or not—to get their wealth in the first place. But one could drive a semitrailer truck through that loophole, as Jerry Rubin did: "All money represents theft. To steal from the rich is a sacred and religious act. To take what you need is an act of self-love, self-liberation."[66] Beyond that, some hippies justified stealing by arguing that capitalism produced economic irrationality and immorality. When surpluses existed in a world of hungry people, stealing from the surplus could not be evil.[67] New York City communard Crescent Dragonwagon made the case straightforwardly: "I honestly believe that if I need something it should be mine, or my family's, and that I shouldn't have to pay for it. I honestly believe that when I go into nearly any store and pay for something *I* am being ripped off. . . . I find 'stealing' to truly be liberating and not stealing at all—liberating not only of goods but of *myself.*" In some cases hippies provided their peers with specific advice on methods of stealing from the corporate thieves.

A series of articles in the *East Village Other* outlined several possibilities: getting free new-account gifts from banks by devious means, "losing" traveler's checks to double one's money, "losing" a credit card, giving false credit card numbers in telephoned business transactions, and flying with airline tickets that had been reported stolen.[68] In several instances, detailed instructions were provided for the fraudulent use of telephone credit card numbers.[69] Most of this information and much more was detailed in Abbie Hoffman's guerilla manual, *Steal This Book.*[70]

One sophisticated form of the rip-off was record and tape bootlegging. Protesting the high prices and alleged monopolistic practices of the record companies, bootleggers sometimes operated in violation of copyright and contractual rights of artists and producers. In most cases their products were of relatively low quality and high price, but the largest, Rubber Dubber Records (with thirty-seven employees), claimed to operate "under a strict code of business ethics" that included the use of only the best vinyl, a guarantee of quality, a price held to six dollars per double album, and the payment of a royalty (twenty-five cents per record) to artists. Rubber Dubber contended that its business was legal, ethical, and necessary to the counterculture.[71]

Hair, Obscenity, Dirt

It might seem frivolous to enunciate an ethic of hair, or profanity, or dirt, but the hippies did just that, largely in self-defense against those who saw hopeless degeneracy in the counterculture's approach to such matters.

Hair was one of the most visible symbols of the culture of opposition. It provided a name of a smash musical about the countercultural lifestyle and the name of at least one underground newspaper (in Minneapolis, circa 1969). Why did hippies grow their hair long? Primarily as a symbol of separateness, or, as Richard Neville put it, as a countercultural declaration of independence.[72] "Long hair, beards, no bras and freaky clothes represent a break from Prison Amerika."[73] Indeed, for some time hippies loved to call themselves "freaks."

The counterculture deemed it equally important to ask why American society was critical of long hair, pointing out that most recent mass murderers were short-haired and that major (especially organized) criminals were usually short-haired and beardless. One writer suggested that the naked ape might possibly feel superior to longhairs because it considered them throwbacks to the earlier stages of the evolution of the species.[74] At any rate, if people worried about the length of things, they would be better advised to concern themselves about the length of the "lying tongues of politicians."[75]

The underground papers generally missed one broader implication of long hair, that of the apparent countercultural tendency toward androgynous appearance.[76] Conscious or not, androgyny was important and helped buttress hip ideas about unity and wholeness. Men grew hair that made them look more feminine, while women wore clothing, especially pants, which had a distinctly masculine air. (It is worth noting here that the counterculture apparently had a lot to do with freeing women to dress in pants. Until the time of the hippies, skirts were the rule for women in all but the most informal settings.)

The historian and philosopher Mircea Eliade once argued that androgyny reflects a dissatisfaction with one's actual situation (cut off from power and divinity) and a wish to recover this lost unity.[77] Thus countercultural androgyny in regard to hair and dress may have reflected the "traditional conception that one cannot be anything *par excellence* unless one is at the same time the opposite."[78]

"Obscene" language was coin of the countercultural realm. The four-letter words first widely used publicly and unabashedly in the hip era were held to have had two main uses: through their shock value they constituted "a symbolic protest against middle-class hypocrisy," and in their frequent explicit sexualness they raised sexual discourse "above the ground in the hope of bringing sex with them—to put sex on the healthful, wholesome, beautiful" plane where it belonged.[79] The Establishment's disdain for "obscenity" helped promote its use in the counterculture, but in any event it soon became so widely used that it simply reflected a rejection of the prevailing social propriety of the day. Hippies believed that society had a misplaced sense of shock:

> What is obscene?
>
> Is it obscene to fuck, or
> Is it obscene to kill?
>
> Is it more obscene to describe fucking,
> An act of love, or

Is it more obscene to describe killing,
An act of hate?

Are pictures of a nude person just fucked
More or less obscene
Than pictures of a dead person just killed?

* * *

Why does the church
Condemn fucking,
An act which creates life, but
Condone killing
An act which takes life?

Why does the church consider it more heinous
For an American soldier to
Fuck
 an eighteen year old unmarried American girl
 than to
Kill
 an eighteen year old unmarried Vietnamese girl
 . . . ?

Why do children learn, at too young an age, that
The biggest no-no in the English language is Fuck
While at the same tender age, or younger, learn that
Hate and kill
Are two of the most acceptable words in the English
 language . . . ?
What is really obscene?
Answer that question, and you will
Discover not only your own true values, but also
Where the true values of our
Christian natures lie.[80]

Finally, hippies were often condemned for appearing to be dirty. Most of them saw bodily dirt as a morally neutral matter, but they perceived substantial irony (or worse) in the fact that their critics were usually among those who consented to pollution, slums, and trash on the airwaves. "That a few Hippies appear dirty punctuates the fact that in a crucial sense all adult non-Hippies are filthy."[81]

Hedonism

A notable difference between the counterethics and conventional Judeo-Christian ethics came at the point of deliberate pleasure. The counterculture maintained as a "basic idea" that "pleasure is good, and not immoral."[82] That had the effect of creating a "hedonistic gap" that, according to Timothy Leary, was "the real problem of the world today."[83] Leary was a notable theoretician of hedonism, proposing to raise the "hedonic index" of persons through "hedonic engineering," which he defined as "designing one's life for pleasure through chemical turn-ons and turn-offs."[84] Hedonism was morally valid, said Leary: it meant "living for pleasure instead of living according to the punishment-reward system that an up-tight society wants to keep us all trapped in."[85]

> An anti-hedonic society is an uptight society, is a punishment society and it's a warlike society, and we just can't afford that any more if we're going to survive as a species.
>
> The only issue today, as in the past, is the hedonic gap. Every issue, whether it's a psychological conflict, personality conflict, or social-political conflict always comes down to a hedonic gap.
>
> Some people try to bring others down or make them feel worse; the innate struggle of every individual is that he wants to feel better.[86]

Leary saw hedonism largely in terms of dope, but others saw it more broadly. Country Joe McDonald once said, "Probably the most revolutionary thing in the U.S. right now is hedonism. By that I don't mean wasting your life away, but doing something that you enjoy. That really puts them uptight."[87] The Sexual Freedom League based much of its rationale for existence on hedonism: "If the pleasure principle is more operative in our lives, the anxiety principle would become less operative. Overall we would be less hostile, more capable of sentiment, affection and love."[88] And if there needed to be a moral justification for hedonism, there were two: the belief that morals were relative, not absolute, and the "saving importance of experience."[89]

William Braden criticized the counterculture at the point of hedonism on strategic grounds: hedonism could enslave as easily as liberate, and a "technetronic dictatorship" could rely on bread and circuses to pacify the masses.[90]

But to the counterculture that was essentially a political argument, a contention that one should deny oneself pleasure for some very hypothetical political possibilities. True hippies could not allow politics to override pleasure.

Truth, Honesty, Simplicity

Paul Krassner once said, "I don't believe in the biblical concept, 'Ye shall know the truth and the truth shall make you free,' because people have such a fantastic capacity to rationalize the truth."[91] That sort of rationalization, which is closely tied to hypocrisy, was consistently one of the main things that the counterculture criticized in majority society. The counterculture saw itself as "struggling to RISE FROM A SOCIETY which has adjusted to levels of moral and intellectual depravity, as low as its level of physical comfort is high."[92] Ralph J. Gleason epitomized the argument:

> Two long-haired kids in a sleeping bag on the fairgrounds is fornication; two crewcut kids after the high school dance in a motel is "sexual experience" and their parents, swapped around in a luxury hotel, is "making love."
>
> It is all right to drink whiskey and run a car into a tree. It is morally wrong to smoke grass and listen to music.[93]

The sin was not so much in the act as in the attitude. The counterculture proposed the elimination of double standards. It proposed a forthright honesty in daily life that it saw sadly lacking in most of society.

Rationality

The counterculture that rejected technology as a god also rejected the Western rationalism that underlies technology. The counterculture proposed an approach to life not of irrationality but of arationality, a disregard of the question of reasonableness. Reason had not answered any of the important questions of life, all of which lay on a plane not inhabited by reason; furthermore, arationality was part of human nature. "Logical argument doesn't work. People's heads don't work logically. People are emotion freaks. People are crazy," Jerry Rubin declared.[94] Symbolically, "Words are the absolute in horseshit," Abbie Hoffman agreed.[95] The counterculture was eros, while Establishment, technological culture was logos. The counterculture was the virgin, technological culture the computer. The counterculture was spirit, technological culture reason.[96] There were not merely minor differences in viewpoint; hippies saw them as symptoms of the vast gulf between the two outlooks on life and culture.

Theodore Roszak wrote at length in forceful refutation of the rational, of objective consciousness, contending that Western culture's insistent dependence on "objectivity" vastly diminished its quality of life and, in fact, hindered a rapport with the world rather than helping it.[97] As Roszak notes, the counterculture was not entirely original in this critique, but helped popularize it: "Theosophists and fundamentalists, spiritualists and flat-earthers, occultists and satanists . . . it is nothing new that there should exist anti-rationalist elements in our midst. What *is* new is that a radical rejection of science and technological values should appear so close to the center of our society, rather than on the negligible margins."[98]

In the counterculture there was little use for objective knowledge (beyond the development of a few simple tools for living, such as cooking, sewing, and primitive building). There was believed to be no overall nature of things in the rational sense. As Paul Goodman put it, everything in the modern world could be reduced to interpersonal relations and power.[99] At that point the fruits of reason turn sour.

Chapter 6
Legacy

Like, two years ago you could walk down the street and see
a guy who looked real weird . . . and you knew. Now, I look
out here and, well, everyone looks weird. You just can't tell
anymore.

—Janis Joplin, *Great Speckled Bird*, July 21, 1969

Decades later, America is a different place than it was in the days of hip. Capitalism and what's-in-it-for-me? values are stronger than ever. The airwaves and blogs are dominated by demagogues who ridicule peace, love, and cooperation. There is no flowering counterculture, no vital New Left, no innovative rock and roll, no generational consciousness—and not much of a sense of enchantment or wonder in any part of society. Peace and love and flower power are no longer standard argot. Methamphetamine has, to a fair degree, supplanted LSD and marijuana; dynamic new music has given way to formulaic sound.

More fundamentally, the imagination that so characterized the sixties, the optimistic and naive anticipation that the world was moving into an age of Aquarian harmony and understanding, seems utterly gone in a time when leading public figures want to clamp down on artistic expression, when the rare political world leader with vision or imagination is relentlessly thwarted by a ruthless and cunning opposition, when cynical materialistic self-indulgence rules the land, when grim environmental realities render the future of the race unpredictable. In many ways hip culture has bloomed and died like a century plant, spectacularly but only once in a lifetime. On the other hand, the new ethics of the hippies has changed the culture in far-reaching ways, even if the vision of revolutionary upheaval has clearly not come to pass.

The Counterethics: Just How New Was It?

The hippies fervently believed that what they were about was something entirely new. The past was rejected, forgotten. With the dawning of the age of Aquarius, an entirely new consciousness was entering the human race, and the hippies were the vanguard of a revolutionary future that would inevitably sweep the world.

The claim that everything hip was new was hardly on the mark, however. Actually, the counterethics had three strata: a reaffirmation of some very traditional ideas and values; a championing of ideas that had been around for some time but were unfamiliar to or unaccepted by the majority; and, yes, some ideas that seem to have been truly original, or at least quite unusual in an American setting.

The reaffirmation of traditional ethical precepts

Much of the counterethics simply reaffirmed time-tested American values and tendencies, albeit sometimes in new clothing. The valuing of community in a country of individualists is an example of that. Americans have always been great champions of individualism. It was in America that the Bill of Rights was adopted, spelling out the rights of the individual to a degree unthinkable to most of the world of two centuries ago and not, conspicuously, specifying where individual rights needed to be bounded for the common good. Yet those individualistic Americans have always been participants, volunteers, community dwellers. As Henry Steele Commager once wrote, "For all his individualism, the American was much given to cooperative undertakings and to joining."[1] The hippies did their own thing, but a key part of the hip vision was generational community.

The hippies were iconoclasts, but iconoclasm is another classic American virtue. Americans early on slaughtered sacred cows—rejecting, for example, traditional government (monarchy), the traditional relationship of church and state, and a formal social class structure. In the nineteenth century, a gaggle of traditional institutions—slavery, the subordination of women, the use of alcohol as a beverage, and others—found themselves under attack by a new generation of reformers. The iconoclasm of the hippies was distinctive only in that new icons came under attack. Slavery and monarchy had already been abolished; the new gods assaulted by the counterculture were rationality, technocracy, and materialism.

Rural romanticism and the desire to protect the earth were also simply new expressions of old instincts. The disavowal of big cities as corrupt and unlivable has been a popular cultural theme for well over a century. Although massive environmental pollution was a new part of the equation in the hip era, the desire to flee to the country was not. The establishment of thousands of communes in rural areas was a replay of the agrarian ideal—not to mention a communal vision—which was well established in the nineteenth century and has continued ever since.[2]

Finally, even in its methodological preference for pursuing social change by appealing to Americans' gut feelings the counterculture was quite traditional. The hippies never worked very hard at trying to change institutions. Their appeal was always to the heart. How do we change society? Well, if enough individuals are transformed, then society will inevitably follow. The hippies were convinced that American society was so degenerate that no scheme of structural changes could possibly succeed. The only hope for a better tomorrow was to drop out, to disaffiliate from society and encourage others to do the same. If enough dropped out, then and only then would a new consciousness dominate society. That appeal—heartfelt and to the heart—is one Americans have made from the beginning.

The espousal of existing minority positions

In rejecting the ideas and values of majority society, the hippies in many cases adopted points of view that had already been articulated by a social minority. In some cases a particular school of thought was thus given wide exposure for the first time, and for that reason the hippies seemed to be proclaiming something really new when they weren't.

Sexual freedom is a case in point. There have long been individuals and groups who have deviated from the established patterns of heterosexuality, monogamy, marriage, and wearing clothes, but they have tended to be few and their voices weak. A free-love movement, while not quite the same thing that would be proclaimed in the days of hip, had a notable following in the nineteenth century.[3] Albert Ellis, to name just one person, wrote and lectured in favor of sexual freedom for decades—although, prior to the coming of the counterculture, ideas like his were hardly the coin of the realm. Similarly there have long been organizations of nudists who have taken off their clothes in the interest of better health and communion with nature, but only with the hippies, for whom nudity meant fun and freedom, did disrobing attract widespread attention.

The hippie precept of dropping out of the larger society to seek a purer life was not a new one, nor was it novel to create communes in the country for those who wanted to live among like-minded dropouts. Certainly some of the early European settlers in America were malcontents who saw themselves as having to withdraw from society and head for the wilderness to find satisfaction. Communes were operating in America from the seventeenth century onward, reaching a major peak in the early to middle nineteenth century. The grand communes of that era were often founded in locations far from major cities and represented dissatisfaction with society's prevailing arrangements. The hippies saw themselves as creating new family structures in their communes, but that had been done fairly extensively in the first half of the nineteenth century. The Shakers, for example, saw themselves as living in families of a new type; "family" was the name of the largest subunit in each of the Shaker villages. The Oneida Community of John Humphrey Noyes saw itself as a single family with hundreds of members; in its system of complex marriage each woman and each man in the community was regarded as a spouse of all the others of the opposite sex.

Finally, the rejection of materialism, consumerism, and the mindless exploitation of the planet were all old themes that prior to the hippies had never had widespread followings. There have always been hermits and members of religious orders who have rejected the dominant culture's material and commercial values, but in possession- and money-mad America they have been few indeed. Similarly there have been those who have argued for the preservation of nature for at least a century and a half, but until recently the majority of Americans have been more interested in conquering than in preserving nature. The hippies were in the line of a cultural vanguard when they argued that the earth needed to be protected, not exploited.

New ethical ideas

Not many ideas are entirely new, but some cherished ethical positions of the hippies were at least distinctive and newly refined. Probably the most important new counterethical position was the positive embrace of "drugs." There have been "drug cults" in other times and places ranging from ancient India to contemporary Native America, but the counterculture took a position new to just about every Euro-American when it argued that heretofore forbidden psychoactive substances could and should be used for pleasure and spiritual insight. (Yes, many have championed the legitimacy of the use of alcohol, America's perennial favorite drug, but it has hardly been argued that alcohol *should* be universally used for exhilaration and introspection.) The hippies believed that dope, universally used, would effect a change of consciousness that would be enormously beneficial to the world. That argument represented a novel point of view.

The promotion of an ethics of fun and play was relatively new in America as well. The Protestant work ethic has dominated the land for centuries. The only people who really aren't expected to work are the rich (and even they would be better off working) and the unfit. In the face of that cultural tradition, the hippies argued that work was not necessary, that modern technological culture was sufficiently productive that it could carry a fair number of nonproducers without undue burden on the rest. Pleasure was no longer to be regarded as demonic; now it was an essential ingredient of the free life. Hedonism, in disrepute in the West perhaps since the time of the Epicureans, was once again an ethical imperative.

Finally, the rejection of rationality and of the whole concept of objective consciousness was an important component of the counterethics, and a distinctive one. There have in the past been anti-rationalists in America, but usually they have opposed only one part of science and/or rationality, as in the case of flat-earthers and six-day creationists, and they have also been socially marginal. The spirit of rationality is so thoroughly embedded in American culture that it can hardly be escaped entirely, but the counterculture worked steadily against it. Devotion to reason, the counterculture argued, has dehumanized life by downplaying emotion. It has made slaves of persons and has essentially contradicted human nature, which is not entirely rational, to say the least.

The Impact of the Counterculture on Society, Then and Now

The hippies were cultural shock troops. Unlike some other dissenters before them, they were often recognizable on sight, with their long hair, flowers and beads, colorful clothing, painted vehicles, and the like. Their ideas were widely if imperfectly known. Suddenly, with widespread public awareness of a counterculture came a huge national debate over recreational drugs, liberated sexuality, rock music, private property, and other topics raised for public debate by the hippies.

Did they have any effect, either transitory or long lasting, on members of society who never considered themselves hippies? Certainly they seem to have had an impact in their own time. It was the hippies who popularized recreational drugs among a wide swath of the population. Dope had been around before, particularly in certain circles of artists and musicians and in various racial subcultures. But never before had it spread so widely through the culture. By 1972 more than 40 percent of the American college student population had tried marijuana, and in all an estimated 24 million Americans had used the illegal weed.[4] Such large populations never tried LSD or other forms of dope, but nevertheless the spread of the smorgasbord of drugs was unprecedented. One survey conducted in 1974 and 1975 found that 22 percent of a national sample of men aged twenty to thirty had used psychedelic chemicals, and 7 percent were using them regularly at the time of the survey.[5] By 1989 one survey concluded that over 70 million Americans, close to 30 percent of the population, had used one or more illicit drugs at some time in their lives, and that nearly 37 million had done so in the previous year.[6]

Although there is some evidence that overall drug use may have declined slightly in the early years of the 2000s (possibly because young people seem to make alcohol increasingly their drug of choice), the Centers for Disease Control and Prevention found that 21 percent of young Americans had used marijuana in 2009, while smaller but still significant numbers had used other illicit substances.[7] Perhaps no greater indicator of a national attitude shift has surfaced than the seemingly steady march toward the legalization of marijuana. In 1996 California legalized medical marijuana in a statewide referendum, and since then some thirteen other states have followed suit. Possession of small amounts of marijuana has been legal in Alaska for some time, and outright legalization looms in several other jurisdictions. Meanwhile, the research on psychedelics that was largely suspended once they became widely used for pleasure has begun again.[8]

Similarly widespread was a new attitude toward sex. Premarital sex became much more widely and openly practiced than ever before, and tolerance of other sexual expressions than genital-to-genital marital heterosex increased substantially. Homosexuals began asserting their rights publicly for the first time. Surveys showed major changes in American attitudes toward sex. As late as 1969 the Gallup Poll found that only 21 percent of American adults approved of premarital intercourse, while 68 percent condemned it, but by the time the new thinking had had a chance to percolate through the culture, that had changed dramatically.[9] A 1977 survey conducted by Yankelovich, Skelly, and White found that only 34 percent of those under twenty-five believed that it was wrong for teenagers to engage in sexual intercourse. Of the whole population, 52 percent believed that it was not morally wrong for an unmarried man and woman to live together, and 56 percent favored civil rights for homosexuals. Asked how their views on sexual morality had changed, 41 percent said that their views had become more liberal, while only 15 percent had become more conservative.[10] That trend has continued into the 2000s, with Americans approving sex between unmarried persons by a three-to-two margin.[11] One dramatic change in American attitudes has been a strong increase in acceptance of rights of homosexuals. Support of gay marriage, to take one notable indicator, has increased to the point that the country will apparently soon have a gay-marriage-supportive majority.[12]

One can argue that sexual liberation would have happened without the hippies. It happened that the hip era came on the heels of such revolutionary cultural developments as the widespread dissemination of oral contraceptives in the early 1960s, the achievement of effective treatment of venereal diseases through antibiotics, and the development of private locations for sexual activity outside the parental home (notably in the universalization of the automobile). Even stipulating the independent emergence of new options, however, the counterculture played an important role in popularizing the new freedom and especially in enunciating the ethics that made it all acceptable.

There were lesser, often transitory impacts as well. For a time in the 1970s hippie ideas about appearance had some influence on the larger society. Longer hair and more colorful clothing for men were in vogue for a few years. Widespread acceptance of casual clothing, especially blue jeans, is now well entrenched. In many circles it is no longer odd to hear once-forbidden four-letter words. But such things were and are peripheral to the central message of the counterculture, except insofar as they represent some general acceptance of the hippie value of self-expressiveness.

The long-term impact of the hippies is not easy to judge. The counterculturists themselves believed that they were on the cutting edge of a true cultural revolution, that the world would be changed forever by the new consciousness they were bringing. As Allen Ginsberg responded when asked in 1969 whether hippies might revert to the middle class as they grew older: "No; impossible. . . . The way's been barred by beatings and arrests. What bridges they haven't burned behind them have been burned for them with pot busts. What's happened to young people is a sudden breakthrough catalyzed in part by psychedelic drugs. Another factor was the deconditioning caused by alienation from social authority as it proved itself completely incomprehensible and mad and burned its own bridges from Hiroshima to Vietnam."[13] One scenario popular among the hippies was that their ultimate cultural triumph was inevitable, that the ideas and ethics of the counterculture would soon predominate in society at large. That vision is the essential point of Charles Reich's *The Greening of America,* a huge best-seller published in 1970.

Naturally, many writers in the hip press expressed the conviction that hip ideas would dominate the world. John Gabree, for example, writing in 1971, saw the counterculture leading the whole society to true peace (a society without war or institutionalized violence), equality, and love (a society that would respect the humanity of everyone, and would celebrate truthfulness and compassion), even if getting there from here still entailed "a hell of a lot of work."[14] And some saw a hip world as simply on its way, hard work or no. As Tom Wolfe wrote, the world seemed to be living with a "millennium at hand, and it *is,* because there's no earthly stopping this thing. It's like a boulder rolling down a hill—you can watch it and talk about it and scream and say Shit! but you can't stop it. It's just a question of where it's going to go."[15]

Others were less optimistic about the ultimate conversion of the world to hip thinking. Nevertheless, they believed that hip would become permanently established as a way of life for an enlightened minority. Raymond Mungo spoke for that position:

> If we live long enough to create it, the New Age will be *peace on earth.* The judicious strife we now suffer on earth must be related to and seen in the light of that Kool Space which will make it an ancient chapter in our development. At the risk of adopting missionary zeal, we ought to go back to the cities and bring out the young and alienated, to the land and peace, "save" them in a sense from the death of the body and soul amid the glitter of better ketchup bottles and new Buicks.
>
> The peace we find in Kool Space will give us the internal strength to move in the Old Age, in the cities, for example, without succumbing to it; the peace in the New mentality is a peace without adequate words ("notoriously non-linear these hippies," says the latest *New York Review*) and we should seek to turn on and carry away the prospective new people rather than merely convince them.
>
> Free from material need, unconcerned for what used to be called "poverty," we will escape the poisons of the city, which itself inhibits our revolution and warps our art. The cities of America are unnecessary evils in an age of electronic communication and transportation; they will become hollow museums to our past, burned down by the poor during the last gasp of the Old Age and now echoing with the sharp footsteps of the occasional, amused visitor. There is Kool Space enough for all of us—*look up today, rather than down.*[16]

Such was the vision, but not exactly the reality. The wave of sixties-nostalgia literature that has appeared over the past few decades has often generally regarded it all as over. There have been endless newspaper feature stories on former hippies who became investment bankers, turned to born-again Protestantism, and acquired trivial but expensive material possessions. The era of the hippies and the New Left was a colorful and chaotic one, but in the long run it hasn't made much of an impact on the larger society: such is the conventional wisdom.

But is that true? Have the changes in American attitudes and activities that apparently followed the heyday of the counterculture vanished? It seems clear enough, as we saw a few pages ago, that by the middle 1970s, in the wake of the counterculture, Americans had become more permissive about sexual activity and drug use. Certainly the hippies had made some impact on style, what with widespread popularity of longer hair on men, colorful and casual clothing, the casual use of once-forbidden words, the evolution of countercultural icons and artifacts (peace signs, coke spoons) into jewelry, and a hundred other things. But has the impact vanished? Is America today no different than it would have been had the legendary generational revolt never occurred? With materialism, capitalism, and sheer greed as rampant in America as they have ever been, is there no legacy at all?

Well, no. Things are not entirely as they were before. There is clearly visible ongoing impact in the three most renowned centers of the hip revolution: sex, dope, and rock and roll. Further, one can make the case that the growing national concern for the environment follows up on an alarm that the hippies were among the first to sound. And the hip rebellion has left its imprint on other parts of American life, such as the spread of the culture of the body and the movement toward socially responsible investing.

As we have seen, Americans continue to be more tolerant of liberal sexual mores than they were before the hippies arrived on the scene, and young people are sexually more active, as a group, than they once were, a pattern that shows no sign of abating. For a time the spread of herpes, and then AIDS, seemed to put the brakes on the sexual revolution, but that retreat from free sexuality seems to have been reversed by the promotion of condom use and the development of drug regimens that make AIDS manageable.

In the case of rock music, it would be hard to argue that the music of the hip era is not still felt today. Indeed, the identical music retains a fair popularity, not only among the aging hippies but among a younger generation: no one who gets into an elevator or visits a grocery store can fail to hear the Beatles or Bob Dylan frequently. When the remaining countercultural bands tour, their concerts are thronged—thousands turned out for Grateful Dead concerts until Jerry Garcia's death in 1995 led to the dissolution of the band, and there is probably no hotter ticket in the business than the Rolling Stones. In the twenty-first century the Stones, Bob Dylan, Joan Baez, Paul McCartney, and many other countercultural musical icons were all touring and still eclipsing everything else musical that had come along in the decades since their rise to popularity. Beyond that, however, the rock that hippies saw as revolutionary has remained the fountainhead of a musical genre that has an enormous following today. Some of it has become unimaginative and formulaic; some of it, such as hip-hop, has gone in directions of its own. Its source in the sixties rock revolution is, however, undeniable.

Other hip themes have continued to resonate in the larger culture. Prominent among them is the cult of the body that at this writing permeates much of America. Hordes of Americans jog and swim and pour into thousands of health centers and buy millions of workout videos. Eating healthy food has gone from being the fanaticism of a few cranks to a concern central to the lives of millions, and organic is the fastest-growing segment of the American food industry, which is struggling to accommodate the surge in demand for the wholesome, chemical-free foodstuffs that are spreading into every supermarket in the land.

Many a suburban family now has food concerns that were once the province of the far-out hippies. Thus there is some plausibility to Craig Dremann's argument that food will be the longest-lasting of all hip innovations: "I can't think of anyone who began eating whole-wheat bread and then went back to white bread. While most of the folks who once thought of themselves as hippies have dropped their overt identification with hippie culture, they still partake of it by the food they eat. They eat hippie food—yogurt, carob, and so on—almost all of which was introduced into the white-bread culture by the original aboriginal hippie culture. . . . I imagine that five hundred years from now about the only lasting cultural contribution that will be attributed to hippies will be the new plant foods and plant uses they introduced."[17]

Growing along with concern for health and nutrition has been the New Age movement, a vague and virtually indefinable collection of spiritual and somatic beliefs and practices with obvious roots in hippie culture (as well as in earlier American metaphysical movements). Many New Age schools focus on spiritual growth. Many of them see spiritual, mental, and bodily growth as necessarily integrated. Practices ranging from massage to the use of crystals to alternative medical treatment to astrology to communication with persons on other planes of existence have wide followings. While some New Age precepts are actually very old, their contemporary popularity seems to have received an important boost from the hippies. The New Age movement is not a very pure preservation of hippiedom. As Andrew Kimbrell has observed, the New Age movement has focused on individual, not social, transformation, and a visionary quest for personal alternatives without compassion for the oppressed is only a fragment, even a parody, of the hip agenda.[18] Nevertheless, the New Age movement is one of the most substantial remnants of hip culture we have.

Other religions have developed American followings since the days of hip as well. Before the hippies most American Buddhists were ethnically Asian, and American Hindus were mostly (East) Indian. Today a wide range of the world's religions have come to have seats at the table of American faith. Not only Buddhism and Hinduism, but also Sufism, Sikhism, Santería, and a host of other religions look like they are here to stay and have followings far beyond their ethnic roots. Who would have thought, before the hippies, that we would have a fully accredited Buddhist university (Naropa University in Boulder, Colorado) in the United States?

Since hippiedom flowered nearly half a century ago, the denizens of the counterculture have now inevitably reached an age when it is necessary to make important financial decisions, especially in planning for retirement. It should not be surprising, therefore, that there is currently a growing movement toward socially responsible investing. The hippies generally proclaimed rather Buddhist ideas about work and money: one should have a right livelihood, and one should use one's resources for the promotion of the good.

In the late 1960s and early 1970s, the question of investments usually focused on college campuses: the demand was that college endowments divest themselves of holdings in businesses selling armaments or operating in South Africa, to cite only two controversial situations. As former hippies and their sympathizers have acquired some assets of their own, they have often clung to the ideal of investing them in a progressive fashion. Whole mutual funds and money-market funds have been created as vehicles for socially oriented investments, and even some major traditional financial firms have begun to cater to this apparently growing market.

A related development is the growth of deliberately socially conscious business enterprises that fairly deliberately try to apply the hip vision to the workplace. Perhaps the best-known example is Ben and Jerry's ice cream company in Vermont. As many articles in the popular press have noted with some wonderment, Ben and Jerry's employees can choose which jobs they want to do, get benefits ranging from profit sharing to college tuition to free ice cream—and work for a company that is serious about its environmental responsibilities and donates 7.5% of its pretax profits to progressive social causes.[19] Other businesses have similar, if less publicized, policies, and many cooperative enterprises (especially natural-food stores) founded during the hip era continue to operate on an alternative business model. The hip vision of meaningful, socially responsible work has not yet swept the country, but it continues to make progress.

To some extent the counterculture could be said to have helped stimulate the rekindled feminist movement of the last third of the twentieth century. The counterculture was largely male defined, but it tried to be inclusive, and caring about people was one of its basic themes. In their broad-spectrum challenge to the prevailing American way of doing things, the hippies did not fail to criticize traditional family life, which inevitably included sharply restrictive ideas about the roles women could play in society. Much of the new feminism of the 1970s was spearheaded by women who had logged at least some time among the hippies, and they reflected the hip critique of mainstream society in their assault on the discrimination women had historically faced.

Perhaps the most enduring legacy of the counterculture is the role that it played in awakening public concern about the environmental crisis of the late twentieth century. The hippies were nature-lovers, and many of them admired the American Indians, whom they saw as, among other things, fine stewards of the natural world. From the beginning one strain—small at first, but vocal—of the hippie critique of American culture was that the country was fouling its nest, that for the sake of profit and convenience the survival of the world itself was severely at risk. As Roderick Nash wrote in *The Rights of Nature,* "One of the most characteristic ideas of the 1960s concerned the need for fundamental changes in American life and thought. At its deepest level, the so-called counterculture advocated a new morality and the wholesale dismantling of many established institutions. The decade began with an emphasis on human rights, but by its end, as perception of an environmental crisis increased, the stakes began to widen to include nature."[20]

The whole notion of the nation's—and the world's—having grave environmental problems was still a new one in the late sixties, and one widely disbelieved. Rachel Carson's *Silent Spring,* the book that first focused widespread attention on the looming environmental catastrophe, had only been published in 1962.[21] Hippies were deeply involved in the first Earth Day, April 22, 1970, and as new and more radical environmental organizations (Greenpeace, Sea Shepherd, Earth First!) began to emerge during and after the hip era, they were often populated by individuals whose consciousness had been raised in the counterculture, and they often took their organizational and strategic cues from the hippies and the New Left. It is a safe guess that today veterans of the counterculture are disproportionately represented in the organizations fighting to turn back the tide of environmental degradation. While one cannot say that the hippies are solely responsible for widespread awareness of the environmental threat, surely their role in sounding alarms was an important one.

In sum, more than a few footprints remain. Progress toward equal rights for African Americans, women, and homosexuals gained a lot of traction in the days of hip. Energy-efficient light bulbs, electric vehicles sold by major auto companies, organic foods, yoga and bodywork, meditation, alternative medicine, casual clothing, recycling, natural childbirth, and, yes, medical marijuana are all fixtures in contemporary society that owe more than a little to the hippies. And beyond those visible things, what subtle legacies remain? As Allen Ginsberg intoned in 1986, "some permanent changes have now been built in so subtly that they are unnoticeable as byproducts of the expansion of mind and the liberation movement of the sixties. So it's the whole cultural change."

Is the Legacy a Nightmare?

Noble ideas can carry seeds of their own destruction. The vision of communal living was inspirational, but the open-door policy adopted by many communes led to their being overwhelmed by deadbeats and even outright thugs who could drive even the most idealistic of the hippies away. Dope might have provided exhilaration and enlightenment, but it often gave way to drugs of the worst sort. Liberated sex and the pursuit of pleasure might have seemed like fun, but such adventures too frequently led to irresponsible behavior, to say the least.

In a time of devastating sexually transmitted diseases and a public badly divided on drug-related issues, was the counterethics simply a curse? Do AIDS and meth and crack and hordes of homeless persons constitute the essential legacy of the counterculture?

No simple answer works very well here. The hippies were key agents in the blossoming of a drug culture, but somehow only part of the hip message managed to penetrate the larger society. The hippies advocated the use of *dope,* but the drugs that seem to be so destructive in America today aren't what the counterculturists called dope. Crack is cocaine, not LSD or marijuana. To the hip ethical theorists, cocaine was one of those things (heroin was another) that entered the scene once acceptance of psychoactive substances had spread widely and helped destroy the visionary world of psychedelia. So hip permissiveness helped open the door to the destruction of hip, as well as to problems elsewhere.

But the shift from dope to drugs does not tell the whole story either. Once dope had been defined, it still had to be used properly: set and setting were crucial components of the experience. Dope trips were ideally taken in positive, supportive company by persons who believed that something akin to religious revelation, or at least something very fun, could come from the experience. By comparison, neither set nor setting is right for the typical user of heroin or crack—or, for that matter, alcohol or the prescription sedatives and tranquilizers that have constituted the largest part of American drug use for many decades. As post-hip editor Mark Satin wrote in 1989, "If the Sixties taught us anything, it is this: Drugs are neither good nor bad. When abused, they can cause great harm. When used properly, they can help us expand our consciousness and enjoy our world."[22]

Further, the hippies would point out that America has lost its perspective in the national crusade against drugs, devoting enormous resources to fighting what is actually a small part of the national drug problem. By any standard the most problematic drug in the country is alcohol, which is used regularly by a substantial majority of adult Americans. According to a study conducted in 1995 and published in 1999, alcohol abuse costs the United States over $175 billion per year (much of that in lost work time and decreased productivity), while all illegal drugs cost the country about $114 billion.[23] According to research published in the *Journal of the American Medical Association* in 2004, alcohol was killing an estimated 85,000 persons per year, while all illicit drugs were killing some 17,000.[24] (Tobacco dwarfs even alcohol here, with an estimated 438,000 deaths per year.)[25]

Finally, the hippies would raise the issue of the nature of the drug *problem,* saying that the *illegality* of drugs is the largest single component of what seems to be regarded today as a national crisis. The view of the majority of Americans, seemingly, is that illicit drugs are wrong because they are illegal, and that they can't be legalized because that would be capitulating to the enemy. That circular logic creates the kind of system in which a terribly destructive drug (alcohol) is legal, while other substances with little destructive potential (peyote, for example) are illegal. While certainly drug use would continue, and possibly increase somewhat, under legalization, much of what is regarded as destructive about drugs would be greatly diminished, as hip observers argued repeatedly. The enormous profit potential of the drug trade would vanish with legalization, and with it the motivation for most of the violence spawned by drugs, which, after all, typically derives from disputes among sellers, not from use. Most hippies believed that legalization would do far more than the outlawing of drugs has to maintain social sanity, and there is little evidence that they would believe otherwise today.

In the case of sex, it is plausible to believe that the sexual liberation of the hip era contributed to the worldwide epidemic of sexually transmitted diseases. Certainly the hippies were public and flamboyant in their pressing of the cause of a radical (by standards previously prevailing) ethics of sex. As

American toleration of and participation in less strict sexual arrangements has spread, so have diseases. (Penicillin may have rendered some diseases unthreatening, but AIDS, herpes, chlamydia, and other stubborn ailments are still very much with us.) One might argue that we are ethically obliged to keep our bodies as healthy as possible, and freewheeling sex does not seem to serve that cause. The hippies argued, however, that freedom and pleasure were key values in the new culture. Would it not then be ethically permissible for one who engaged in sexual activity with eyes wide open to (and condom in place to minimize) potential health risks to choose pleasure over health?

The arrival of AIDS would not affect the basic ethical equation. The stakes are higher for AIDS, obviously, than for other sexually transmitted diseases. One's moral obligation to protect and inform one's partners becomes towering here, but the most basic ethical issue—is it right (or at least morally permissible) to have sex outside of heterosexual marriage?—is not changed by the advent of a new disease.

Certainly there are other seeming casualties of sexual freedom than disease. High divorce rates and great numbers of unwanted children born to single parents, for example, would seem to be sour fruits of freer sex. As with drugs, however, the hippies would argue, viewing the contemporary scene, that the countercultural message has been distorted and acted out irresponsibly. Freedom to engage in sexual activities once widely disapproved of does not mean that one is no longer responsible for one's actions. Using birth control and otherwise behaving responsibly were never condemned by the hippies.

Did the Hippies Create a Disastrous Backlash?

One could argue that the hippies' net long-term accomplishment was negative, that a backlash to hip excesses arose that boosted a new conservatism that left the hip vision in the ashcan. After all, a decade later there was a vocal, active New Right in America, a religio-political movement that helped turn American politics in a profoundly conservative direction. The rise and continuing impact of hard-line conservatism in American social and political life is a given. It is, however, difficult to figure out just how much of the social liberalization so distasteful to the New Right came from the hippies and how much came from other sources, such as New Deal liberalism. For that matter, one could debate how much of the rise of the right came as a backlash to 1960s-era exuberance and how much arose independently, as the product of, for example, well-funded politicians and charismatic electronic media demagogues.

The religious wing of the New Right has anathematized free sex, illegal drugs, secular rock music, world peace through love and understanding, communal sharing, and many other cherished hippie values. But the list of condemned liberalizations included many more items than those especially championed by the hippies. Jerry Falwell, a key New Right leader through the 1980s and beyond, was quoted as saying that the largest single element in his own movement into political activism, in which he moved from the traditional independent Baptist stance of rejecting and avoiding the corrupt secular world to advocacy of political involvement, was the *Roe vs. Wade* Supreme Court decision affirming free choice on abortion.[26] The hippies by and large supported women's access to abortion, but they were hardly major players on the pro-choice scene. (Ironically, some of the early players in liberalizing abortion laws were secular conservatives who, in a manner that smacked more than a little of racism, saw easy abortion as population control for people who might need social services.)[27] Hippies were also little involved in other causes that seemed to provoke the New Right, such as the growth of the welfare state and the secularization of the public schools.

The New Right arose as a backlash against half a century of liberalization of social mores and ideals. The hippies were a part of that liberalization process, serving as highly visible agents for some of it. They were certainly prominently in the public eye for several years, and they aroused enormous animosity among some conservatives. To the extent that they irritated the New Right, the hippies undermined their own goals. Just how much they abetted the rise of the New Right, however, is a judgment call.

Outposts: Where Hip Still Survives

Perhaps the best place to see some survival for the counterculture is in a few scattered enclaves. In some smaller cities, most of them college towns, and in quiet rural encampments life goes on. Not many would claim the title "hippie" today, but more than a few are still living the life.

The larger cities seem to have sheltered relatively few who continue to try to maintain hip ways. Perhaps the necessity for a substantial cash income and the ongoing degradation of urban life are among the causes of that. One still sees long hair on men often enough, and sixties-style clothing; surely the ingestion of psychoactive substances has not ceased. But cities are not great places for tuning in and dropping out.

Urban hip survival, such as it is, is probably best found in the booming New Age movement, which was discussed a few pages ago. "Movement" is an ambitious term here, because the New Age is utterly amorphous, and New Agers themselves disagree enormously as to where to draw the boundary lines. Broadly, the movement involves mind and body, everything from massage to mental self-abnegation. New Age schools offer degrees and certificates in a myriad of fields from transpersonal psychology to water-witching. The New Age movement owes much to the hippies, those cultural revolutionaries who bucked tradition and explored the hidden fringes of contemporary life.

The hip subculture endures more identifiably in smaller places. Many college towns throughout the country have managed to accommodate persons who still live at least somewhat counterculturally. In those places some children of hip have tried to work countercultural ideals into the social and physical fabric, as by operating businesses specializing in alternative energy or organic living, or by promoting community projects such as recycling and reducing use of automobiles. Persons with hip values have congregated in several such centers, particularly on the West Coast. One who visits the Oregon Country Fair or the Saturday Market in Eugene, Oregon, for example, may well feel as if he or she were in the Haight-Ashbury circa 1967.

The other most important locus of preservation of sixties idealism is the ongoing communitarian movement. Today they are usually called intentional communities, not communes, but hundreds have survived from the hip era, and hundreds of new ones have been formed since then on similar patterns. Now as then no one is able to count the communities, but many are there, with a population probably in the tens of thousands. Some freewheeling, secular communities have managed to overcome steep odds and keep themselves alive, even thriving; for example, Twin Oaks, near Louisa, Virginia, has lasted for over four decades and has reportedly never been healthier.[28] Several religious communes have also survived. What is sometimes regarded as the archetypal hippie commune, the aforementioned Farm community in Summertown, Tennessee, is still very much alive. Although enormous financial problems in the early 1980s led to an abandonment of important parts of the communal structure and to substantial depopulation, some 200 persons still live there, many of them continuing in their vows of simplicity and community. The Farm still embraces several projects that reflect classic hip idealism, such as Plenty, a foundation that does relief and development work in the United States and abroad, and the Ecovillage Training Center, which offers courses in permaculture, environmentally sound building construction, and sustainable living generally.

The gospel of alternative sexuality continues to be lived in some hip outposts. A movement known as polyamory has arisen in post-hip times, dedicated to making the case for multiple sexual partners. Some polyamorists practice "polyfidelity," a system of shared partners in which one is to remain absolutely faithful to the group, but within the group rotates among partners, sometimes on a predetermined schedule.

So hip life goes on in a few enclaves. More significantly, it goes on in the lives of many who remain touched by the vision they experienced in the 1960s era. As one commented to me, "I think our culture is in much better shape than it used to be. There is more diversity; things are more interesting. I am absolutely convinced that people accept one another more openly than they did before the hippies arrived; there is less prejudice in our society than ever before. Sure, some hippies have become insurance salesmen, but none of them that I know deny that what they did was very good. I still believe the things I believed then. We all learned some things then that will be with us for the rest of our lives."[29] Importantly, few of those who lived the hip life regret having done so. In the 1990s I directed a project that interviewed several hundred former (and ongoing) residents of hip communes. Most were still living in socially responsible ways, and most were still following the Buddhist precept of right livelihood—teachers, nurses, writers, artists, and an occasional lawyer working for a nonprofit. We asked them if they regretted having lived countercultural lives, and whether they would do it again, given the opportunity. Many weren't so sure about going back to hip in later life, but virtually all were glad they had done it and had plenty of happy memories.[30]

Notes

Introduction to the Second Edition

1. J. L. Simmons and Barry Winograd, *It's Happening* (Santa Barbara, CA: Marc-Laird Publications, 1966), 12–15.

2. William C. Shepherd, "Religion and the Counter Culture—A New Religiosity," *Sociological Inquiry* 42.1 (1972): 7–8.

3. Chester Anderson, "God Works through Harry Anslinger," *Los Angeles Free Press*, Apr. 26, 1968.

4. "Youth: The Hippies," *Time,* July 7, 1967, 20.

5. Ibid., 22.

6. Steven M. Tipton, *Getting Saved from the Sixties: Moral Meaning in Conversion and Cultural Change* (Berkeley: Univ. of California Press, 1982), 14.

7. Theodore Roszak, *The Making of a Counter Culture* (Garden City, NY: Doubleday, 1969).

8. David Carter, ed., *Allen Ginsberg: Spontaneous Mind: Selected Interviews 1958–1996* (New York: HarperCollins, 2001), 440.

9. John Gruen, *The New Bohemia* (New York: Grosset and Dunlap, 1966).

10. Norman Mailer, "The White Negro," in *Voices of Dissent* (New York: Grove, 1958), 199, 200, 206.

11. "The Declaration of Cultural Evolution," *East Village Other,* late May 1968 (illegible date). Authorship is not credited, but an earlier issue of *EVO* (about the middle of May—illegible date) stated that Leary, Ginsberg, Krassner, and Hoffman were working on the statement.

12. Art Johnston, "A Theory of Hip; Part One: 'What Have You Got?'" *Fifth Estate,* Nov. 15–30, 1966.

13. Jean-Jacques Lebel, "Counter Culture: Hip Culture Ripped Off," *Spectator,* Dec. 8, 1969.

14. Lawrence Lipton, "Radio Free America," *Los Angeles Free Press,* May 3, 1968.

15. Raymond Mungo, *Total Loss Farm: A Year in the Life* (New York: Dutton, 1970), 18.

16. Steve Haines, "To Build a Nation," *Berkeley Tribe,* Nov. 7–13, 1969.

17. Walt Crowley, "Constipated Counter-Attack Catharsis," *Helix,* Sept. 19, 1969.

18. Roszak, *Making of a Counter Culture,* 24.

19. Jack G. Burgess, "Notice to the Dead and Dying: You Are Standing on a Generation," *Los Angeles Free Press,* Apr. 25, 1969.

20. George D. Maloney, "On Bridging the Generation Gap—Can We Work It Out?" *Spokane Natural,* Aug. 16–29, 1968.

21. Andrew Kopkind, untitled article, *Rolling Stone,* Sept. 20, 1969.

22. Laurence Leamer, *The Paper Revolutionaries: The Rise of the Underground Press* (New York: Simon and Schuster, 1972), chap. 4.

23. Paul Goodman, *New Reformation* (New York: Random House, 1970), chap. 4.

24. Richard Neville, *Play Power* (London: Jonathan Cape, 1970), 18.

25. Kenneth Westhues, using the term "counterculture" to comprehend any dissenting subculture, concluded from his research that "the most basic condition for the rise of a counterculture is perceived discrepancy between societal ideology and lived experience." See Kenneth Westhues, *Society's Shadow: Studies in the Sociology of Countercultures* (Toronto: McGraw-Hill Ryerson, 1972), 141.

26. P. G. Stafford, "Acid, Rock and Revolution," *Seed* 2.10 (1968).

27. Stan Iverson, "To Touch the Genitals," *Helix,* Oct. [?] 1968.

28. Quoted in Mayer Vishner, "Rock and Revolution," *Win,* Dec. 15, 1968, 20–21.

29. Roszak, *Making of a Counter Culture,* 66.

30. Goodman, *New Reformation,* 202.

31. See Norman Mailer, *The Armies of the Night* (New York: New American Library, 1968).

32. "Changes" (a dialogue among Alan Watts, Timothy Leary, Allen Ginsberg, and Gary Snyder), *San Francisco Oracle* 1.7 (1967). The specific quotation is attributed to Leary.

33. Mick Wheelock, "Is Love Dead?" *Los Angeles Free Press,* Nov. 22, 1968.

34. Raymond Mungo, *Famous Long Ago: My Life and Hard Times with Liberation News Service* (Boston: Beacon, 1970), 53.

35. Ralph J. Gleason, "Perspectives: Is There a Death Wish in U.S.?" *Rolling Stone,* Apr. 5, 1969.

36. Mungo, *Famous Long Ago,* 168.

37. Interview with Bob Maurice, *Great Speckled Bird,* May 4, 1970.

38. David Super-Straight, "Some Notes on the Violent Generation," *Berkeley Barb,* Aug. 1–7, 1969.

39. Mungo, *Famous Long Ago,* 134–35.

40. Greil Marcus, "The Woodstock Festival," *Rolling Stone,* Sept. 20, 1969.

41. Attributed to Bill Finn in "No Time for Sex," *Berkeley Barb,* Feb. 4, 1965.

42. "Marxist Scholar Opines on Hips" (interview with George Novack of the Socialist Workers Party), *Berkeley Barb,* May 12–18, 1967.

43. "The Revolution Is Now!" *Spokane Natural,* Aug. 16–29, 1968. Originally published in *Liberation;* distributed via Liberation News Service.

44. David McReynolds, "An Open Letter to: Richard Alpert," *Win,* July 1967, 10–12.

45. "Marcuse on the Hippie Revolution," *Berkeley Barb,* Aug. 4–10, 1967.

46. Andrew Kimbrell, "The Coming Era of Activism: New Left Meets New Age," *Utne Reader* no. 26 (Mar.–Apr. 1988): 66.

47. "Warning to So-Called 'Paper Panthers,'" *Black Panther,* Sept. 14, 1968, 10.

48. Harvey Cox, "God and the Hippies," *Playboy* 15.1 (Jan. 1968): 94.

49. Shepherd, "Religion and the Counter Culture," 3.

50. "'Clear Light' Sought for LSD Religionists," *Berkeley Barb,* June 17, 1966.

51. Ralph J. Gleason, "Perspectives: Are We Lost in a New Dark Age?" *Rolling Stone,* Dec. 13, 1969.

52. "Headitorials," *Spectator,* Jan. 7, 1969.

53. Steve Russell, "An Open Letter to the Kampus Krusade," *Rag,* Nov. 23, 1970.

54. "Jesus Was a Militant," *Great Speckled Bird,* Feb. 2, 1970.

55. Thaddeus and Rita Ashby, "Did Jesus Turn On?" *Berkeley Barb,* Dec. 23, 1966.

56. Laurence Leamer argued that the underground press was the only "broad, unifying institution" the counterculture produced. See Leamer, *Paper Revolutionaries,* 13.

57. The three available collections are the Underground Press Collection (AMS Press), made available to member institutions by the Center for Research Libraries in Chicago; a collection compiled and distributed by University Microfilms of Ann Arbor; and the Bell and Howell Underground Press Collection, which includes papers published between 1965 and 1970, the years during which the underground press rose and flourished.

58. Abe Peck, *Uncovering the Sixties: The Life and Times of the Underground Press* (New York: Pantheon, 1985), xvi–xv.

Chapter 1
The Ethics of Dope

1. Tom Coffin, "Dope," *Great Speckled Bird,* Oct. 6, 1969.

2. "Dope Summit Conference," *Dallas Notes,* Apr. 2–15, 1969.

3. Quoted in Norman Hartweg, "Psychedelic Prophet Alpert to Speak in Los Angeles," *Los Angeles Free Press,* Sept. 3, 1965.

4. Jan Hodenfield, "It Was Like Balling for the First Time," *Rolling Stone,* Sept. 20, 1969.

5. Mungo, *Total Loss Farm,* 71.

6. "Dr. Timothy Leary" (excerpts from a debate at the University of Utah), *Electric Newspaper* 1.2 (1968).

7. "Psychiatrist Says Teens Who Don't Smoke Pot Are 'Sick,'" *Hips Voice,* Apr. 15, 1970.

8. "Poll Indicates 69% Have Used Grass," *University Daily Kansan,* Oct. 8, 1971.

9. Cited in Peter Stafford, *Psychedelic Baby Reaches Puberty* (New York: Praeger, 1971), 27.

10. "Drug Use Not Abating, Study Shows" (National College Poll), *Lawrence (KS) Daily Journal-World,* Nov. 15, 1972.

11. National Commission on Marihuana and Drug Abuse, *Marihuana: A Signal of Misunderstanding* (Official Report of the National Commission on Marihuana and Drug Abuse) (New York: New American Library, 1972), 39.

12. Lewis Yablonsky, *The Hippie Trip* (New York: Pegasus, 1968), 346–47.

13. According to one report, marijuana arrests increased from 6,800 in 1963 to 23,952 in 1966; the amount of marijuana seized by border officials increased from 6,444 pounds to 23,716 pounds during the same period. Source: FBI crime reports, cited in "Bust Measurements," *Marijuana Review,* Oct.–Dec. 1969.

14. Hodenfield, "It Was Like Balling for the First Time."

15. "Intergalactic Union Dopogram," *East Village Other,* Aug. 11, 1970. Originally published in *Scanlan's,* Aug. 1970.

16. "Vice-President's Daughter Caught with Marijuana," *Los Angeles Free Press,* Sept. 5, 1969.

17. National Commission on Marihuana and Drug Abuse, *Marihuana: A Signal of Misunderstanding,* 38.

18. See Martin A. Lee and Bruce Schlain, *Acid Dreams: The CIA, LSD and the Sixties Rebellion* (New York: Grove Press, 1985).

19. Helen Swick Perry, *The Human Be-In* (New York: Basic Books, 1970), 73.

20. Hal Cromley, quoted in Ben Fong-Torres, "Feds' Dope Circus: 'How Much LSD Do You Take to Be Addicted?" *Rolling Stone,* Nov. 29, 1969.

21. "Pot Conference in Buffalo," *East Village Other,* Mar. 14, 1969.

22. Attributed to Phil Melman in Robert Novick, "Phil Melman Busted at 75," *San Francisco Express-Times,* Mar. 7, 1968 (via Liberation News Service).

23. Mike Scudder, "High School Drugs," *Buffalo Chip,* Nov. 1968.

24. "Shit as a Household Word," *Berkeley Barb,* Sept. 19–25, 1969.

25. The Rev. Stanley J. Keach, "Thoughts on the Drug Scene," *Speak Easy* 1.6 (1968).

26. Tom Coffin, "Everybody's Talkin,'" *Great Speckled Bird,* Sept. 22, 1969. On this point, see also Timothy Miller, "Drug Bust in Kansas," *Christian Century* 88.11 (Mar. 17, 1971): 332–33.

27. "Leary and Alpert: Turn On/Tune In/Drop Out," *Berkeley Barb,* June 24, 1966.

28. Ken Anderson, "Dope," *Hartford's Other Voice,* Sept. 25, 1969.

29. "Heads Revolting," interview with Art Kleps, *Berkeley Barb,* Dec. 20–26, 1968. (Originally published in *Real Free Press.*)

30. [Stephen Gaskin], *Hey Beatnik! This Is the Farm Book* (Summertown, TN: Book Publishing Co., 1974), unpaginated.

31. Allen Ginsberg, "The Great Marijuana Hoax," *Atlantic Monthly* 218.5 (Nov. 1966). Reprinted in the *Electric Newspaper* 1.2 (1968).

32. Ronald Broudy, "Don't Legalize Pot," *Rat,* Apr. 19–30, 1968.

33. Howard Moody, "Heroin: The Law Is Worse Than the Drug," *Village Voice,* Sept. 14, 1972.

34. Ralph Metzner saw two common elements in all the dope churches: the need on the part of many individuals to structure the dope experience on the assumption that structured and/or ritualized use of dope produced a better experience, and the need to provide social self-protection in a fashion similar to that of a labor union. ("An Interview with Ralph Metzner," *Seed,* Aug. 11–25, 1967.)

35. Richard Alpert, (illegible title), *San Francisco Oracle,* Jan. 1967.

36. Interview with Timothy Leary, *Yarrow Stalks,* no. 1 (1967).

37. Timothy Leary, "Head Line," *Rag,* Jan. 9, 1967. (Originally published in the *San Francisco Oracle.*)

38. Timothy Leary, "The Politics, Ethics, and Meaning of Marijuana," in *The Marihuana Papers,* ed. David Solomon (New York: New American Library, 1966), 130.

39. Timothy Leary, *High Priest* (New York: World, 1968), flyleaf.

40. Timothy Leary, "Head Line," *Rag,* Jan. 9, 1967. (Originally published in the *San Francisco Oracle.*)

41. Art Kleps (interviewed by Joe Dana), "The New Gurus," *Oracle of Southern California,* Dec. 1967.

42. Peter Novick, "Underground God," *Washington Free Press,* Mar. 19, 1968.

43. "Heads Revolting," *Berkeley Barb*, Dec. 20–26, 1968. (Originally published in the *Real Free Press*.)

44. Art Kleps, *The Boo Hoo Bible* (San Cristobal, NM: Toad Press, 1971).

45. Art Grosman, "Interview with a 66 Year Old Peyote Eater," *Washington Free Press*, July 16–30, 1968.

46. For the Shiva Fellowship Church, see "A Temple of Cannabis," *Rolling Stone*, Nov. 1, 1969; for the Psychedelic Venus Church, see "Sex Drug Cult," *Berkeley Tribe*, Nov. 27–Dec. 5, 1969; for the Fellowship of the Clear Light, see "Clear Light not Bright," *Berkeley Barb*, July 8, 1966; for the American Council of Internal Divinity, see "The Gossiping Guru," *San Francisco Oracle* 1.6 (1967); for the Psychedelic Peace Fellowship, see "Psychedelic Peace Fellowship," *Oracle of Southern California*, Oct. 1967.

47. Michael Kindman, "On This Cube I Will Build My Church," *Fifth Estate*, Jan. 1–15, 1967.

48. "Intergalactic Union Dopogram," *East Village Other*, Aug. 11, 1970. (Originally published in *Scanlan's*, Aug. 1970.)

49. "Leary and Alpert: Turn On/Tune In/Drop Out," *Berkeley Barb*, June 24, 1966.

50. Tuli Kupferberg, "The Hip and the Square," *Berkeley Barb*, Aug. 4–10, 1967.

51. Will Albert, "Who Is Mary Jane?" *Notes from the Underground*, Aug. 15–31, 1967. (Originally published in the *Paper*.)

52. Timothy Leary offered this definition of the religious experience: "The religious experience is the ecstatic, incontrovertibly certain, subjective discovery of answers to four basic spiritual questions," which are the Ultimate-Power question ("What is the Ultimate Power of [*sic*] Basic Energy which moves the universe, creates life? What is the cosmic plan?"), the Life question ("What is life, where did it start, where is it going?"), the Human-Destiny question ("What is man, whence did he come, and where is he going?"), and the Ego question ("What am I? What is my place in the plan?"). See Timothy Leary, "The Religious Experience: Its Production and Interpretation," *Journal of Psychedelic Drugs* 1.2 (Winter 1967): 7.

53. "Windcatcher," *Good Times*, Aug. 7, 1969.

54. "Sacraments are catalysts rather than ends. Anything one gets from the marijuana experience was there all the time, only perhaps unexplored." Will Albert, "Who Is Mary Jane?" *Notes from the Underground*, Aug. 15–31, 1967. (Originally published in the *Paper*.)

55. "Start Your Own Religion," *Oracle of Southern California*, June 1967.

56. Mel Lyman, "To All Who Would Know," *Seed* 2.1 (1968). (Originally published in the *Avatar*.)

57. "Black Market Research," *Notes on Pot* (*Dallas Notes*), Feb. 16–29, 1968; "Dope Quiz Results," *Fifth Estate*, Apr. 1–15, 1968.

58. Paul Krassner (interview), "LSD, Revolution and God," *San Francisco Oracle* 1.6 (1967).

59. Leary, "The Religious Experience," 6.

60. R. E. L. Masters and Jean Houston, *The Varieties of Psychedelic Experience* (New York: Dell, 1966), 265.

61. Walter Houston Clark, *Chemical Ecstasy* (New York: Sheed and Ward, 1969), 62.

62. "The Attractions of LSD," *Washington Free Press*, Mar. 7, 1968.

63. Walter N. Pahnke, "Drugs and Mysticism: An Analysis of the Relationship between Psychedelic Drugs and the Mystical Consciousness," PhD diss., Harvard Univ., 1963.

64. "Bishop Pike: Interview," *Helix*, Sept. 29, 1967. In a similar vein, Walter Houston Clark has written that drugs are "always a factor" in religious experience "if we could admit as 'drugs' those powerful biochemicals, more often called hormones, which are natural in the human body and without whose involvement no act of human consciousness, sacred or profane, can occur." Clark, *Chemical Ecstasy*, 7–8.

65. Allen H. Reid, "An Open Letter on Drugs to Swami Satchidananda," *Hips Voice*, Aug. 26, 1970. Reid was replying to the swami's contention that drugs cannot be a way to true mystical insight.

66. "Why Psychedelics?" *Oracle of Southern California*, Aug. 1967.

67. Stafford, "Acid Rock and Revolution."

68. Shepherd, "Religion and the Counter Culture," 6.

69. "Shiva Missionary and Cop Go Up in Cloud of Smoke," *Berkeley Barb*, June 14–20, 1968.

70. "The Noblest of All Human Professions: Clear Light," *Berkeley Barb*, Dec. 18–24, 1970. (Originally published in *Georgia Straight*.)

71. "Shit as a Household Word," *Berkeley Barb*, Sept. 19–25, 1969.

72. "Intergalactic Union Dopogram," *East Village Other*, Aug. 11, 1970. (Originally published in *Scanlan's*, Aug. 1970.)

73. P. G. Stafford, "Acid Rock and Revolution—Part II," *Seed* 2.11 (1968).

74. R. Gordon Wasson has established that the *soma* of ancient India was the Amanita Muscaria, a psychoactive mushroom. (See R. Gordon Wasson, *Soma: Divine Mushroom of Immortality* [New York: Harcourt, Brace and World, 1969].) The same mushrooms may have been a key ingredient in the Elusinian mysteries, one of the forerunners of contemporary secret societies. (See Masters and Houston, *Varieties of Psychedelic Experience*, 251.)

75. Thaddeus and Rita Ashby, "Did Jesus Turn On?" *Berkeley Barb*, Dec. 23, 1966.

76. John Allegro, *The Sacred Mushroom and the Cross* (London: Hodder and Stoughton, 1970), xx.

77. Gridley Wright, "Strawberry Fields Forever . . . ?" *Oracle of Southern California,* Aug. 1967.

78. Paul Scorpio, "LSD and Me (Part III)," *Distant Drummer,* Mar. 26, 1970.

79. Timothy Leary, "Playboy Interview," *Playboy* 13.9 (Sept. 1966). Reprinted in the *Los Angeles Free Press,* Sept. 1–7, 1967.

80. "Black Market Research," *Notes on Pot* (*Dallas Notes*), Feb. 16–29, 1968; "Dope Quiz Results," *Fifth Estate,* Apr. 1–15, 1968.

81. "Aquarius, M. D.," *Great Speckled Bird,* Nov. 3, 1969.

82. William Braden, *The Age of Aquarius* (Cleveland: Quadrangle Books, 1970), 237–47. This thesis is also supported by Philip Slater, *The Pursuit of Loneliness: American Culture at the Breaking Point* (Boston: Beacon, 1970), chap. 1.

83. Alex Forman and F. P. Salstrom, "Revolution, Diggers Style," *Distant Drummer,* Oct. 3–10, 1969.

84. "Tompkin Square Smoke-In," *East Village Other,* Aug. 5–17, 1967.

85. Claudia McCarthy, "A Search for Self," *Old Mole,* May 29–June 11, 1970.

86. Walt Crowley, "Those Vegematic Blues," *Helix,* Apr. 30, 1970.

87. Andrew Weil, *The Natural Mind* (Boston: Houghton Mifflin, 1972), 96–97.

88. Timothy Leary, introduction to *LSD: The Consciousness-Expanding Drug,* ed. David Solomon (New York: G. P. Putnam's Sons, 1964), 18–21.

89. Timothy Leary, Ralph Metzner, and Richard Alpert, *The Psychedelic Experience* (New Hyde Park, NY: University Books, 1964), 11.

90. Ibid.

91. "Shit as a Household Word," *Berkeley Barb,* Sept. 19–25, 1969.

92. Jean Raisler, "Placid on Acid," *Berkeley Tribe,* Aug. 29–Sept. 4, 1969.

93. "Black Market Research," *Notes on Pot* (*Dallas Notes*), Feb. 16–29, 1968; "Dope Quiz Results," *Fifth Estate,* Apr. 1–15, 1968.

94. John Rosevear, "Dope Smoking—The State of the Art," *Los Angeles Free Press,* June 14, 1968.

95. According to Howard Moody, a Massachusetts court once held that alcohol relieved tension and was otherwise beneficial in effect, but that marijuana could only be used for pleasure and could therefore constitutionally be outlawed. In effect, the court said that drug-enhanced pleasure equaled abuse. See Moody, "Heroin," 20.

96. Weil, *The Natural Mind,* 17.

97. "Black Market Research," *Notes on Pot* (*Dallas Notes*), Feb. 16–29, 1968.

98. See, for example, the statement of Dr. Bernard Rascombe, "Psychiatrist Says Teens Who Don't Smoke Pot Are 'Sick,'" *Hips Voice,* Apr. 15, 1970.

99. Eugene Schoenfeld, M.D., "Does LSD Really Harm?" *Florida Free Press,* June 30, 1968.

100. Thane Gower Ritalin, "The Hippies and the Hypocrites," *Seed,* Aug. 11–25, 1967.

101. Many scholarly books and articles on the medical applications of marijuana and LSD had appeared by the time of the flowering of hip. One important work on the medical uses of LSD is *The Use of LSD in Psychotherapy and Alcoholism,* ed. H. A. Abramson (Indianapolis: Bobbs-Merrill, 1967). See also Albert A. Kurland, M.D., "The Therapeutic Potential of LSD in Medicine," in *LSD, Man and Society,* ed. Richard C. DeBold and Russell C. Leaf (Middletown, CT: Wesleyan Univ. Press, 1967).

102. See, for example, Robert Novick, "Phil Melman Busted at 75," *San Francisco Express-Times,* Mar. 7, 1968 (via Liberation News Service); "The Attractions of LSD," *Washington Free Press,* Mar. 7, 1968.

103. "Marijuana as Medicine," *Los Angeles Free Press,* Mar. 20, 1970 (via Liberation News Service).

104. "Black Market Research," *Notes on Pot (Dallas Notes),* Feb. 16–29, 1968; "Dope Quiz Results," *Fifth Estate,* Apr. 1–15, 1968.

105. Ginsberg, "The Great Marijuana Hoax," as reprinted in the *Electric Newspaper* 1.2 (1968).

106. Lawrence Lipton, "The High Priest of LSD," *Los Angeles Free Press,* Oct. 4, 1968. (Originally published in *Paris Review.*)

107. Lois Lane, "Leary Love Rap," interview, *Berkeley Barb,* Dec. 26, 1969–Jan. 2, 1970.

108. David Faber, "Smack Down," *Argus,* Feb. 9–23, 1970.

109. Robert Claiborne, "Buying Time and Safety: Let's Legalize Heroin," *Village Voice,* Dec. 16, 1971.

110. Allen Ginsberg, "Mafia and Junk," *Los Angeles Free Press,* May 22, 1970. (Originally published in *Good Times.*)

111. "Leary Speed Warning," *Kaleidoscope,* Feb. 13–26, 1970.

112. "Allen Ginsberg on Speed, Etc.," *Distant Drummer* 1.9 (1968). (Originally published in the *Electric Newspaper.*)

113. David Faber, "Smack Down," *Argus,* Feb. 9–23, 1970.

114. *Dallas Notes,* Oct. 15–Nov. 4, 1969.

115. "Peanut Butter Spreads," *Spokane Natural,* Nov. 7–20, 1969.

116. "I Saw the Best Minds of My Generation," interview with Allen Ginsberg, *East Village Other,* Mar. 14, 1969.

117. "Aquarius M.D.," *Great Speckled Bird,* Sept. 22, 1969.

118. Tom Coffin, "Everybody's Talkin,'" *Great Speckled Bird,* Sept. 22, 1969.

119. In 1989 Kesey said, "I never dosed anybody. I never gave anybody drugs without telling him. It's rape. You can't violate a person like that. I have been dosed by people trying to impress me. I can't tell you how much I hate it." See John Lehndorff, "Kesey Takes in Life with a 60's Slant," *Wichita Eagle*, Sept. 17, 1989, 2E.

120. Timothy Leary, "Dope," *Electric Newspaper* 1.3 (1968).

121. Art Kunkin, "A Personal Statement by the Publisher on Acid Testing," *Los Angeles Free Press*, Apr. 11, 1969.

122. Allen Ginsberg, "Renaissance or Die," *San Francisco Oracle*, Jan. 1967.

123. See Ed Sanders, *The Family* (New York: Dutton, 1970).

124. Lawrence Lipton, "Radio Free America," *Los Angeles Free Press*, Jan. 19, 1970.

125. David E. Smith, "Life with Manson," *Berkeley Barb*, Jan. 16–22, 1970.

126. Sanders, *The Family*, 69ff. Sanders dealt especially with the Process Church of the Final Judgment ("an English occult society dedicated to observing and aiding the end of the world by stirring up murder, violence and chaos, and dedicated to the proposition that they, the Process, shall survive the gore as the chosen people") as the largest and most dangerous offender; his criticisms were sufficiently incisive (and insufficiently substantiated) that under the threat of a lawsuit he dropped the material from his "revised" paperback edition. However, many years later he was still privately claiming that his charges were entirely true (personal communication). The former Process Church has been through many transformations since; some members reconstituted their movement as the Foundation Church of the Millennium, later known as the Foundation Faith of God.

127. Untitled statement by Mel Lyman, *American Avatar* (undated), 1969.

128. David Felton, "The Lyman Family's Holy Siege of America," *Rolling Stone*, Dec. 23, 1971, and Jan. 6, 1972.

129. Lucian K. Truscott IV, "Chop, Chop: Age of Psychedelic Fascism," *Village Voice*, Oct. 14, 1971.

130. Bruce Hoffman, "Yogi Hits Weed for Binding Users to 'Valley of Illusions,'" *Los Angeles Free Press*, Oct. 3, 1969.

131. Allan Cohen, quoted in "Meher Baba Tells It," *Screw*, Jan. 1, 1969. (Originally published in *Oz*.)

132. Allen H. Reid, "An Open Letter on Drugs to Swami Satchidananda," *Hips Voice*, Aug. 26, 1970.

133. Allen Ginsberg, "Allen and the Maharishi," *Florida Free Press*, June 30, 1968. (Originally published in the San Francisco *Express-Times*.)

134. Bill Drew and Mike Rosen, "Waukegan Kids," *Connections*, Dec. 11, 1968–Jan. 15, 1969.

135. "The Revolution Is Now!" *Spokane Natural,* Aug. 16–29, 1968. (Originally published in *Liberation;* distributed by Liberation News Service.)

136. "David Crosby of the Byrds," *Oracle of Southern California,* Oct. 1967.

137. Ron Norman, "An Open Letter from One Hippie," *Seventy-Nine Cent Spread,* Nov. 5, 1968.

138. David Faber, "Smack Down," *Argus,* Feb. 9–23, 1970.

139. "Mike Curb and Richard Nixon Battle Dopers," *Rolling Stone,* Nov. 26, 1970.

Chapter 2
The Ethics of Sex

1. The National Organization for Women was formed in 1966; most other new feminist groups were formed in 1968 or thereafter. The major books that defined the movement were almost all published in 1970 or later. See Lois W. Banner, *Women in Modern America: A Brief History,* 2d ed. (San Diego: Harcourt Brace Jovanovich, 1984), 254–55.

2. John Cunnick, "Dump Truck Baby," *Helix,* Nov. 2, 1967.

3. Goodman, "The New Reformation," 147.

4. Leah Fritz, "Female Sexuality and the Liberated Orgasm," *Berkeley Tribe,* Oct. 16–23, 1970.

5. Albert Ellis saw several correlations between activism and liberated sexuality. See Albert Ellis, "Sex and Revolution: How Are They Related?" *Other Scenes,* Aug. 1970.

6. "In Search of the Erotic," *Good Times,* Dec. 4, 1970.

7. Dave Wilson, "Scaramouche," *Haight-Ashbury Maverick* 1.4 (1968). (Originally published in *Avatar.*)

8. "Sex in Spokane," *Spokane Natural,* Dec. 8, 1967.

9. Don H. Somerville, "Sexology," *Helix* 9.9 (1969).

10. Colleen Houlihan, "A Chick on Sex," *Walrus* 2.4 (1968).

11. "On 'n' Off on Zensible Sex," *Berkeley Barb,* Mar. 18, 1966.

12. See P. N. Dedeaux, "Sade Lib," *Village Voice,* May 13, 1971; Terry Kolb, "Masochist's Lib," *Village Voice,* May 13, 1971; Harold Nederland, "Asexuals Have Problems Too," *Village Voice,* Feb. 25, 1971; Howard Smith, "Scenes," *Village Voice,* Apr. 22, 1971.

13. "Very Pleasurable Politics," *Rat,* Dec. 17, 1970–Jan. 6, 1971.

14. Wilson, "Scaramouche."

15. See, for example, "Gentlemen . . . The Queen," *Berkeley Barb,* May 10–16, 1968.

16. One underground writer told of a game called S.E.X. being sold in Berkeley: "a total non-stop adult sex game where two, three, or four couples roll the dice to

determine who does what to who. S.E.X. takes over where strip poker left off."
See John Wilcock, "Other Scenes," *Berkeley Barb,* Dec. 5–11, 1969.

17. About the only sexual preferences questioned even occasionally in the hip world were pornography and sexual devices, such as vibrators. One writer contended, "Sexual liberation is not achieved with gadgets and machines that temporarily eliminate the boredom of conventional sexuality. Fuck books or orgy movies will not teach us to relate to one another in a new, equal, giving, non-possessive manner." Pam Gwin, "Buy, Sell, Don't Smell," *Great Speckled Bird,* Dec. 15, 1969.

18. Bob Cummings, "Total Sexuality," *Rag,* June 19, 1969. (Originally published in *Modern Utopian.*)

19. Somerville, "Sexology."

20. See Allan D. Coult, "Sex, Religion, and LSD," *Oracle of Southern California,* Jan. 1968.

21. The most comprehensive case for an ethics of homosexuality was "A Gay Manifesto," written by Carl Wittman. See *Los Angeles Free Press,* Aug. 14, 1970. This manifesto was widely reprinted in the underground press.

22. Dan Borroff, "Gay Is Beautiful," *Hips Voice,* May 27, 1970. (Originally published in *Seed.*)

23. Ellen Breiter, "In Ancient Greece You Were 'Queer' If You Weren't Homosexual," *Willamette Bridge,* May 29–June 4, 1970. The title of the article overstates the actual situation, but the idealization of man-boy love and practice of homosexuality more generally in the ancient world is well attested. See, for example, Daniel H. Garrison, *Sexual Culture in Ancient Greece* (Norman: Univ. of Oklahoma Press, 2000), chap. 6.

24. "Gay Lib," *Argus* 2.5 (1970). (Originally published in *Rat.*)

25. Jefferson Poland, "So Try It!!!" *Berkeley Barb,* June 19–25, 1970.

26. The Sandman, "Get Gay!!" *Berkeley Tribe,* Oct. 20–Nov. 6, 1970.

27. Carl Wittman, "A Gay Manifesto," *Los Angeles Free Press,* Aug. 14, 1970.

28. Bill Wingell, "A Time for Holding Hands," *Distant Drummer,* July 10, 1969.

29. Don Jackson, "Brother Don Has a Dream," *Los Angeles Free Press,* Aug. 14, 1970.

30. Many also advocated legislation permitting homosexual marriages. Such marriages did occur publicly at least by 1969, although of course they did not have the sanction of the state. See "Wedding Rights," *Berkeley Barb,* Apr. 18–24, 1969.

31. Leo E. Laurence, "Gay Page," *Berkeley Tribe,* Nov. 21–28, 1969.

32. T. R. Wayne-Hill, "Houston Homosexual Speaks Out," *Space City News,* Oct. 11–25, 1969.

33. Quoted in "Mattachine International," *Great Speckled Bird,* Oct. 6, 1969.

34. Wayne-Hill, "Houston Homosexual Speaks Out."

35. "Gay Revolution Comes Out," *Rat,* Aug. 12–26, 1969.

36. "Beast and the Beauty," *Helix,* July 18, 1968.

37. LeRoy Moore Jr., "From Profane to Sacred America," *Journal of the American Academy of Religion* 39.3 (Sept. 1971): 333.

38. Ibid., 333.

39. Gina Shepard, "If It's Their Thing Just Let 'em Leer," *Berkeley Barb,* July 7–13, 1967.

40. Michael Stanley, "Let It All Hang Out," *Los Angeles Free Press,* Oct. 11, 1968.

41. See, for example, "Fun-A-Nude," *Kaleidoscope,* June 7–20, 1968; "Campus Nudity," *Helix* 7.10 (1969).

42. Neville, *Play Power,* 80.

43. Stanley, "Let It All Hang Out."

44. "What's Nudes?" *Spokane Natural,* Feb. 28–Mar. 13, 1969 (via Liberation News Service). This incident, with an accompanying explicit photograph, was widely reported in the underground press.

45. Sue Marshall, "Pot-Sex Church Celebrates Hedonism," *Los Angeles Free Press,* Mar. 13, 1970.

46. "Sex is not practiced religiously. It is more of a happening" (Yablonsky, *Hippie Trip,* 23).

47. Shepard, "If It's Their Thing Just Let 'em Leer."

48. "The Om United Nude Brigade," *Rolling Stone,* July 23, 1970.

49. Phil Pukas, "Omigod," *Berkeley Barb,* June 12–18, 1970.

50. "OMM," *Berkeley Barb,* June 5–11, 1970.

51. "Guru Ginsberg's Little Homilies on Holy Nudity," *Berkeley Barb,* June 14–20, 1968.

52. Marshall, "Pot-Sex Church Celebrates Hedonism."

53. Leo Laurence, "Doin' It on the Altar," *Berkeley Tribe,* Jan. 2–9, 1970. Some Gay Liberation Front members were upset by the publication of this description, since it represented a position not all of them were willing to take. See Leo E. Laurence, "Gay God Squad," *Berkeley Tribe,* Jan. 9–15, 1970.

54. Sexually transmitted diseases were on a sharp upward curve during the hip era. 362,502 cases were reported in 1955; that figure jumped to 628,812 in 1969 and 693,606 in 1970. Although the number of cases of syphilis declined greatly with the advent of antibiotic drugs, the incidence of gonorrhea, the most common sexually transmitted disease in hippie days, increased even more sharply. See the *Statistical Abstract of the United States, 1972,* 93d ed. (Washington, DC: Bureau of the Census, 1972), 77.

55. Dov Witz, "Don't Applaud the Clap—or—You Only Hurt the One You Love," *Seed* 1.7 (1967).

56. Rick Strauss, "The Clap," *Oracle of Southern California*, Aug. 1967.

57. Wilson, "Scaramouche."

58. Interview with Timothy Leary, *Yarrow Stalks*, no. 1 (1967).

59. See, for example, Kristal Higrass, "Choosing a Method," *Seed* 2.9 (1968).

60. Twig Daniels, "Abortion!" *Buffalo Chip*, Dec. 1968.

61. Mary Hamilton, "Survival in the Jungle—Number Eight," *Rat*, Sept. 10–23, 1969.

62. Women's Liberation Health Collective, "Women, Abortion, and Health Care," *Rat*, Dec. 25, 1968–Jan. 7, 1970.

63. Paul Krassner and Ken Kesey, "An Impolite Interview with Ken Kesey," *Realist* no. 90 (May–June 1971): 47.

64. [Stephen Gaskin], *Hey Beatnik! This Is the Farm Book* (Summertown, TN: Book Publishing Co., 1974), unpaginated.

65. "Hooray for Orgies," *Berkeley Barb*, May 13, 1966.

66. "Sex Freedom League Aims Clarified," *Berkeley Barb*, Apr. 15, 1966.

67. "More Nude Happenings for Berkeley," *Berkeley Barb*, Feb. 25, 1966.

68. "'Enjoy, Enjoy' Sex Duet's Spring Tune," *Berkeley Barb*, Apr. 22, 1966.

69. Leo E. Laurence, "SFL—Not Just Fucking Around," *Berkeley Tribe*, Aug. 29–Sept. 4, 1969.

70. Jaakov Kohn, "Interview with Tim Leary," *Rag*, June 12, 1969. (Originally published in the *East Village Other*.)

71. Quoted in "SCUM Manifesto," *Connections*, Feb. 5–20, 1969.

72. Judith Brown, "Women's Liberation," *Great Speckled Bird*, Nov. 11, 1968. (Originally published in the *Southern Patriot*.)

73. Vivian Estellachild, "Hippie Communes," *Women: A Journal of Liberation* 2.2 (1970): 40–41.

74. Tiresias, "A Kiss on the Mouth," *Berkeley Barb*, Jan. 23–29, 1970.

75. Martha Shelley, "Stepin Fetchit Woman," *Seed* 5.2 (1970).

76. Peggy Persephone and Robin of Arc, "Witch Power," *Rat*, Nov. 15–28, 1968.

77. Ibid.

78. Sherrie Rubin, "Hymens for Husbands," *Everywoman*, June 19, 1970.

79. Marion Meade, "Women and Rock: Sexism Set to Music," *Women: A Journal of Liberation* (Fall 1970): 24–26.

80. "Women Take Over Rat," *Rat*, Feb. 6–23, 1970.

81. Peck, *Uncovering the Sixties*, 213.

82. Robin Morgan, "Goodbye to All That," *Rat*, Feb. 6–23, 1970.

83. Jefferson Fuck Poland, "Is Berkeley Fucking?" *Berkeley Barb,* Apr. 10–16, 1970.

84. Tom Hayden, "Tom Objects," *Berkeley Barb,* Oct. 18–24, 1968.

85. Bill Stanley, "The Pseudo-Sexual Revolution," *Walrus,* Mar. 1, 1970.

Chapter 3
The Ethics of Rock

1. Chester Anderson, "Notes from the New Geology," *San Francisco Oracle* 1.6 (1967).

2. Geoffrey Stokes, "The Sixties," in Ed Ward, Geoffrey Stokes, and Ken Tucker, *Rock of Ages: The Rolling Stone History of Rock and Roll* (New York: Simon and Schuster, 1986), 252.

3. Ron Jarvis, "When the Mode of the Music Changes," *Space City!* Jan. 17–30, 1970.

4. John Sinclair, "Rock and Roll Dope," *Fifth Estate,* June 4–18, 1968.

5. Ibid., Nov. 28–Dec. 11, 1968.

6. "[I]t really isn't a very good idea to abstract rock lyrics from the accompanying music for isolated scrutiny. Rock is essentially an appeal to the gut sense of rhythm, intensely energy-releasing and sexual. In this respect rock magnifies the condition of all poetry." (Karen Murphy and Ronald Gross, "All You Need Is Love. Love Is All You Need," in *Pop Culture in America,* ed. David Manning White [Chicago: Quadrangle, 1970], 206.)

7. Sinclair, "Rock and Roll Dope."

8. Anderson, "Notes from the New Geology."

9. Jon Landau, "Rock 1970," *Rolling Stone,* Dec. 2, 1970.

10. Generally, the counterculture's position on rock technology reflects its position on technology as a whole. Steve Levine, an editor of the *San Francisco Oracle,* was asked by Leonard and Deborah Wolf how the counterculture could reconcile its objections to technology with the necessity of technology for rock; his response was that the objection was never so much to technology itself as to its uses. (See *Voices from the Love Generation,* ed. Leonard Wolf [Boston: Little, Brown, 1968], 55.)

11. Charles Reich, *The Greening of America* (New York: Random House, 1970), 245.

12. Quoted in Jack Hutton, "The Rolling Stone Interview: Ringo," *Rolling Stone,* Feb. 10, 1968.

13. Stafford, "Acid Rock and Revolution—Part II."

14. Ron Jarvis, "When the Mode of the Music Changes," *Space City!,* Jan. 17–30, 1970. The MC5, incidentally, eventually reversed its stand and bowed out of revolutionary rock.

15. Jonathan Eisen, quoted in Joseph Ferrandino, "Rock Culture and the Development of Social Consciousness," in *Power to the People: New Left Writings,* ed. William Slate (New York: Tower, 1970), 177.

16. Interview with Country Joe McDonald, *Good Times,* Oct. 23, 1969.

17. Unsigned letter to the editor, *Rag,* Oct. 12, 1970.

18. Plato, *Republic,* Book III, 401 (my translation).

19. Ralph J. Gleason, "Songs Would Do More Than Books," *Rolling Stone,* Mar. 1, 1969.

20. Ralph J. Gleason, "Festival Paranoia," *Rolling Stone,* Sept. 6, 1969.

21. Ralph J. Gleason, "Fighting Fire with Fire: An End to Logic," *Rolling Stone,* May 28, 1970.

22. Ellen Sander, "Dear Abbie," *Los Angeles Free Press,* Sept. 5, 1969.

23. Arthur Johnson, "Music as God," *Distant Drummer,* Dec. 12–25, 1968.

24. Irwin Silber, "The Topical Song 'Revolution' and How It Fizzled Out," *Heterodoxical Voice,* Nov. 1968. (Originally published in the *Guardian.*)

25. Edward Taub, "A Heavyweight Fades," *North Carolina Anvil,* July 18, 1970.

26. Simmons and Winograd, *It's Happening,* 158.

27. James T. Carey, "The Ideology in Popular Lyrics: A Content Analysis," in Westhues, *Society's Shadow,* 99.

28. Ibid., 109.

29. "Violence, Psychedelics, and Cultural Revolution—Now," *Rag,* July 3, 1969. (Originally published in *Georgia Straight.*)

30. Ralph J. Gleason, "Bob Dylan and the Children's Crusade," in *Conversations with the New Reality,* ed. Ramparts editors (San Francisco: Canfield Press, 1971), 72.

31. "The Rolling Stone Interview: Bob Dylan," *Rolling Stone,* Jan. 20, 1968.

32. Jonathan Cott, "The Rolling Stone Interview: John Lennon," *Rolling Stone,* Nov. 23, 1968.

33. John Vicente, "A Beatle Meets the Press" (George Harrison interview), *Oracle of Southern California,* Aug. 1967.

34. Jon Landau, "Rock 1970," *Rolling Stone,* Dec. 2, 1970.

35. David Satterfield, "Country Music in America (Part I)," *Spectator,* Nov. 11, 1969.

36. "Rock Rip-Off," *Seed* 4.10 (1969).

37. Thorne Dreyer, "Love and Haight," *Rag,* June 5, 1967.

38. Henry P. Dankowski, "Beggars' Banquet," *Berkeley Tribe,* Dec. 12–19, 1969.

39. "The View from the Mud," *Rolling Stone,* Aug. 6, 1970.

40. Gary Thiher, "Woodstock: Escape from Amerika," *Rag* 3.28 (1969).

41. Max Lerner, quoted by Hodenfield, "It Was Like Balling for the First Time."

42. Greil Marcus, "The Woodstock Festival," *Rolling Stone,* Sept. 20, 1969.

43. "Woodstock," *Space City News,* Aug. 28–Sept. 11, 1969. (Via Liberation News Service.)

44. Andrew Kopkind, untitled article, *Rolling Stone,* Sept. 20, 1969.

45. John Hilgardt, "That Aquarian Exposition," *East Village Other,* Aug. 20, 1969.

46. "A Murderous Thing," *Berkeley Barb,* Dec. 12–18, 1969.

47. Many different versions of the story of the employment of the Hell's Angels have circulated. For an overview account of the Altamont concert, see Stokes, "The Sixties," 445–46. For a variety of perspectives on the concert and its meaning, see *Altamont: Death of Innocence in the Woodstock Nation,* ed. Jonathan Eisen (New York: Avon, 1970).

48. See, for example, George Paul Csicsery, "Stones Concert Ends It," *Berkeley Tribe,* Dec. 12–19, 1969.

49. "Leary Love Rap," *Berkeley Barb,* Dec. 26, 1969–Jan. 2, 1970.

50. "A Stony Thing," *Berkeley Barb,* Dec. 12–18, 1969.

Chapter 4
The Ethics of Community

1. Roy Ald, *The Youth Communes* (New York: Tower, 1970), 140.

2. Rosabeth Moss Kanter, *Commitment and Community: Communes and Utopias in Sociological Perspective* (Cambridge: Harvard Univ. Press, 1972), 245.

3. Jules Siegel, "West of Eden," *Playboy* 17.11 (Nov. 1970): 174.

4. Benjamin Zablocki, *The Joyful Community* (Baltimore: Penguin, 1971), 300.

5. Keith Melville, *Communes in the Counter Culture* (New York: William Morrow, 1972), 23.

6. Judson Jerome, *Families of Eden: Communes and the New Anarchism* (New York: Seabury, 1974), 16–18.

7. On Drop City see Mark Matthews, *Droppers: America's First Hippie Commune, Drop City* (Norman: Univ. of Oklahoma Press, 2010). Incidentally, the reader should be warned that a novel called *Drop City,* by T. C. Boyle (New York: Viking, 2003), has nothing to do with the pioneer commune in Colorado. Its title notwithstanding, the book is based on Morning Star Ranch, with bits of Olompali Ranch and other communes thrown in, and has been vigorously denounced as demeaning and inaccurate by former residents of both the real Drop City and Morning Star.

8. David Satterfield, "Country Music in America (Part III)," *Spectator,* Dec. 2, 1969.

9. "Woodstock," *Space City News,* Aug. 28–Sept. 11, 1969. (Via Liberation News Service.)

10. Greil Marcus, "The Woodstock Festival," *Rolling Stone,* Sept. 20, 1969.

11. Benjamin DeMott, "Rock as Salvation," in White, *Pop Culture in America,* 199–200.

12. Reich, *Greening of America,* 244–245.

13. Anderson, "Notes from the New Geology."

14. Sinclair, "Rock and Roll Dope."

15. Tuli Kupferberg, "The Coming Catastrophic Age of Leisure," in *Counter Culture,* ed. Joseph Berke (London: Peter Owen, 1969), 82.

16. John Sinclair, quotation on cover of paper, *Berkeley Tribe,* July 17–24, 1970.

17. Stanley Krippner and Don Fersh, "Communes," *Other Scenes,* Oct. 1970.

18. J. R. Kennedy, "Communes," *Fifth Estate,* Aug. 6–19, 1970.

19. Gene Carlson, "Birth of a Tribe," *Oracle of Southern California,* Nov. 1967.

20. Gorkin, "Notes from New Mexico," *Rag,* July 10, 1969. (Originally published in the *Village Voice.*)

21. William C. Shepherd, "Counter Cultural Religiosity: A Reply to Bellah, Baum, and Lidz," *Sociological Inquiry* 42.2 (1972): 171.

22. Ed Schwartz, "Why Communes Fail," *Fusion,* Nov. 12, 1971, 25.

23. Robert Houriet, *Getting Back Together* (New York: Coward, McCann and Geohegan, 1971), 73.

24. Keith Melville saw the surge of hippies toward communalism as beginning in roughly 1966–67, arguing that the counterculturists had found both urban life and radical activism wanting by then. See Keith Melville, *Communes in the Counter Culture* (New York: William Morrow, 1972), 22.

25. Mungo, *Total Loss Farm,* 73.

26. Mungo, *Famous Long Ago,* 114.

27. "Fooman Zybar," *Washington Free Press,* May 1–15, 1969.

28. Hodenfield, "It Was Like Balling for the First Time."

29. "Did Mad Moment Mar Beautiful Leary Lecture?" *Berkeley Barb,* Feb. 21–27, 1969.

30. Mungo, *Total Loss Farm,* 99.

31. After many local struggles, Gottlieb deeded Morningstar Ranch to God, helpfully agreeing to continue paying the taxes on it himself. Soon a lawyer went to court to have the ranch attached to satisfy a debt: his client had suffered a lightning loss in Phoenix that had been ruled "an act of God" and therefore not subject to compensation from the insurance company involved. Suddenly, however, God had assets within the reach of the law. See "God Named Party in Property Suits," *Rolling Stone,* July 12, 1969.

32. Haines, "To Build a Nation."

33. Wavy Gravy, *Something Good for a Change: Random Notes on Peace Thru Living* (New York: St. Martin's, 1992), 164–71.

34. Allen Ginsberg, untitled interview, *Fifth Estate,* Apr. 1–15, 1968.

35. Interview with Timothy Leary, *Yarrow Stalks,* no. 1 (1967).

36. Schwartz, "Why Communes Fail," 22–23.

37. Michael Traugot, *A Short History of the Farm* (Summertown, TN: Author, 1994).

38. Stanley Krippner and Don Fersh, "Communes," *Other Scenes,* Oct. 1970.

39. Kit Leder, "Women in Communes," *Win,* Mar. 15, 1970, 14–16. (Originally published in *Women: A Journal of Liberation.*)

40. Estellachild, "Hippie Communes," 43.

41. Marilyn Foster et al., "How We Live as Toads," *Women: A Journal of Liberation* 2.2 (1970): 45.

42. Schwartz, "Why Communes Fail," 24.

43. Quoted in John Humphrey Noyes, *History of American Socialisms* (New York: Hillary House, 1961 [1870]), 653–54.

44. Gene Carlson, "Birth of a Tribe," *Oracle of Southern California,* Nov. 1967.

45. Schwartz, "Why Communes Fail," 25.

46. David E. Smith, "Life with Manson," *Berkeley Barb,* Jan. 16–22, 1970.

47. See, for example, Slater, *Pursuit of Loneliness,* 148.

48. "Talking About My Generation," *Great Speckled Bird,* June 15, 1970.

49. Slater, *Pursuit of Loneliness,* 149–50.

50. Gene Carlson, "Birth of a Tribe," *Oracle of Southern California,* Nov. 1967.

51. Slater, *Pursuit of Loneliness,* 5.

52. Hodenfield, "It Was Like Balling for the First Time."

53. "On the Subject of Music," *Avatar,* Jan. 19–Feb. 1, 1968.

54. Gorkin, "Notes from New Mexico," *Rag,* July 10, 1969. (Originally published in the *Village Voice.*)

55. Mungo, *Total Loss Farm,* 151.

56. Goodman, "The New Reformation," 146.

57. Timothy Leary, "You Are a God, Act Like One," *Mile High Underground* (Fall 1967).

Chapter 5
Forward on All Fronts

1. Cal Steinmetz, "On Bein' at the Be-In," *Berkeley Barb,* Jan. 20, 1967.

2. "Youth: The Hippies," *Time,* July 7, 1967, 20.

3. Lionel H. Mitchell, "Look at Down Here," *East Village Other,* June 15–July 1, 1967. Other underground writings strikingly resemble Christian treatises on ideal love; see, for example, "Aquarian Beat," *San Francisco Oracle* 1.6 (1967).

4. Ron Norman, "An Open Letter from One Hippie," *Seventy-Nine Cent Spread,* Nov. 5, 1968.

5. Mitchell, "Look at Down Here."

6. Les Wall, "All the Lonely People," *Walrus,* Oct. 15–30, 1968.

7. Tuli Kupferberg, "The Love of Politics and the Politics of Love," *Berkeley Barb,* Apr. 12–27, 1967.

8. Ellen Sander, "Dear Abbie," *Los Angeles Free Press,* Sept. 5, 1969.

9. The Diggers received a great deal of publicity in the early days of the counterculture, but then faded from the scene. Some have suggested that only the publicity changed; the term "Digger" fell into disuse, but their activity continued. See Alex Forman and F. P. Salstrom, "Revolution, Diggers Style," *Distant Drummer,* Oct. 3–10, 1969.

10. "Diggers," *Oracle of Southern California,* July 1967.

11. Cal Steinmetz, "On Bein' at the Be-In," *Berkeley Barb,* Jan. 20, 1967.

12. "For Love Not Lucre," *Berkeley Barb,* Nov. 25, 1966; "Just Plain Holy Water," *Berkeley Barb,* Nov. 22–28, 1968.

13. Sam Allen, in a letter to the editor of *Rolling Stone;* quoted with approval in "Quote of the Week," *East Village Other,* Feb. 18, 1970.

14. "Thudpucker Raps," *Dallas Notes,* July 2–15, 1969.

15. "Hippies: Death on a Sunny Afternoon," *Rolling Stone,* Nov. 9, 1967.

16. Jeff Jassen, "Love Community, Conspiracy Clash," *Berkeley Barb,* Mar. 10, 1967.

17. Jeff Jassen, "What Price Love," *Berkeley Barb,* May 5–11, 1967.

18. "Is Love Obscene," *Berkeley Barb,* May 26–June 1, 1967. (Originally published in the *Canadian Free Press.*)

19. Philip Slater wrote that "the fundamental political goal of the new culture is the diffusion of power, just as its fundamental economic goal is the diffusion of wealth." Slater saw such diffusion as both realistic and practical. See Slater, *Pursuit of Loneliness,* 145–47.

20. Mungo, *Famous Long Ago,* 77.

21. Mungo, *Total Loss Farm,* 40.

22. Slater saw that problem as a manifestation of the "compulsive American tendency to avoid confrontation of chronic social problems"—that is, we try "to solve long-range social problems with short-run 'hardware' solutions. . . . Our approach to social problems is to decrease their visibility." See Slater, *Pursuit of Loneliness,* 12, 15.

23. "Roving Rat Fink," *Berkeley Barb*, Jan. 3–9, 1969.

24. Nick Tosches, "Getting Out the Vote," *Fusion*, Nov. 26, 1971, 31.

25. Iverson, "To Touch the Genitals."

26. Quoted in Braden, *Age of Aquarius*, 276.

27. Gleason, "Perspectives: Is There a Death Wish in U.S.?"

28. Mungo, *Famous Long Ago*, 168–69.

29. Sun Eagle, "Summer Solstice—New Mexico," *East Village Other*, Sept. 10, 1969.

30. Anderson, "God Works through Harry Anslinger."

31. George Harrison, quoted in Nick Jones, "The Rolling Stone Interview: George," *Rolling Stone*, Feb. 10, 1968.

32. "A Letter Appeal," *San Francisco Oracle* 1.11 (1967).

33. See Paul Scorpio, "LSD and Me (Part II)," *Distant Drummer*, Feb. 5–12, 1970.

34. Reich, *Greening of America*, 7.

35. Yablonsky, *Hippie Trip*, 57.

36. Timothy Leary, "Declaration of Evolution," *East Village Other*, Sept. 8, 1970; Leonard Magruder, "A Middle Aged Beatnik among the Hippies," *Notes from the Underground*, Jan. 17–31, 1968.

37. "Leary and Alpert: Turn On/Tune In/Drop Out," *Berkeley Barb*, June 24, 1966.

38. "Dropouts Delight," *San Francisco Oracle*, Jan. 1967.

39. Clark, *Chemical Ecstasy*, 121–22.

40. Gary Thiher, "Woodstock: Escape from Amerika," *Rag* 3.28 (1969).

41. Lipton, "Radio Free America."

42. Alan Watts, "Manifesto to Cut the Big Hang-Up," *East Village Other*, Jan. 1–15, 1968.

43. Alan Watts, "Wealth versus Money," *Playboy* 15.12 (Dec. 1968): 214.

44. Walter Bowart, "Casting the Money Throwers from the Temple," *East Village Other*, Sept. 1–15, 1967.

45. Jerry Rubin, "Rubin Raps: Money's to Burn," *Berkeley Barb*, Jan. 19–26, 1968.

46. Maureen Orth, "Giving $14,905 Away: A Hip Soap Opera," *Village Voice*, Oct. 21, 1971, 5, 8.

47. Mungo, *Total Loss Farm*, 106.

48. Jerry Rubin, "And in America We Are All Learning to Become Vietcong," *Berkeley Barb*, Jan. 5–11, 1968.

49. Kenneth Keniston, *Young Radicals: Notes on Committed Youth* (New York: Harcourt, Brace and World, 1968); quoted in Braden, *Age of Aquarius*, 59.

50. Mungo, *Total Loss Farm*, 105.

51. Neville, *Play Power,* 19.

52. Johan Huizinga, *Homo Ludens: A Study of the Play Element in Culture* (London: Routledge and Kegan Paul, 1949).

53. Neville, *Play Power,* 273–74.

54. Ibid., 274.

55. Ron Jarvis, "When the Mode of the Music Changes," *Space City!* Jan. 17–30, 1970.

56. Allen Ginsberg, "Playboy Interview," *Playboy* 16.4 (Apr. 1969): 240.

57. Abbie Hoffman and Jaakov Kohn, "Abbie," *East Village Other,* May 14, 1969.

58. Slater, *Pursuit of Loneliness,* 46.

59. Reich, *Greening of America,* 242.

60. Neville, *Play Power,* 263.

61. Kupferberg, "Coming Catastrophic Age of Leisure," 85.

62. Slater, *Pursuit of Loneliness,* 103. Slater (97) went so far as to say that scarcity (rather than, say, age) and attitudes regarding it comprised the heart of the difference between the counterculture and majority culture.

63. David Ramsay Steele, "Abolish Money," *Washington Free Press,* May 16–31, 1969.

64. Westhues, *Society's Shadow,* 208.

65. Victor Jasha, "Why Drugs," *Rag,* Jan. 27, 1970.

66. Rubin, *Do It!* (New York: Simon and Schuster, 1970), 122.

67. Neville, *Play Power,* 269–70.

68. Frank Ferris, "Rip-Off," *East Village Other,* Oct. 27 and Nov. 3, 10, and 17, 1970.

69. See, for example, "Ma Bell Tapped," *Berkeley Tribe,* Dec. 31, 1971–Jan. 6, 1972.

70. Abbie Hoffman, *Steal This Book* (New York: Grove, 1971).

71. Brian Kirby, "Yours Truly, Rubber Dubber," *Los Angeles Free Press,* Nov. 12, 1970.

72. Neville, *Play Power,* 18.

73. Jerry Rubin, *We Are Everywhere* (New York: Harper and Row, 1971), 42.

74. Clay Geerdes, "Is Long Hair a Psycho-Sexual Threat to the State?" *Los Angeles Free Press,* May 30, 1969.

75. Thane Gower Ritalin, "The Hippies and the Hypocrites," *Seed,* Aug. 11–25, 1967.

76. Theodore Roszak wrote briefly of the tendency toward cultivation of "a feminine softness" among countercultural males, but, like most other writers, did not pursue androgyny in depth. See Roszak, *Making of a Counter Culture,* 74.

77. Mircea Eliade, *Mephistopheles and the Androgyne* (New York: Sheed and Ward, 1965), 122.

78. Ibid., 110.

79. "Obscenity," Washington *Free Press,* Feb. 29, 1968. (Originally published in the San Diego *Door).*

80. John Sieler, in *Asterisk* (Omaha), quoted by Ethel Grodzins Romm, *The Open Conspiracy* (Harrisburg, PA: Stackpole Books, 1970), 36.

81. Thane Gower Ritalin, "The Hippies and the Hypocrites," *Seed,* Aug. 11–25, 1967.

82. Jean Raisler, "Placid on Acid," *Berkeley Tribe,* Aug. 29–Sept. 4, 1969.

83. Quoted in "High Priest Points Ahead to Happy Era," *Berkeley Barb,* Feb. 14–21, 1969.

84. Quoted in Jean Raisler, "Placid on Acid," *Berkeley Tribe,* Aug. 29–Sept. 4, 1969.

85. "High Priest Points Ahead to Happy Era," *Berkeley Barb,* Feb. 14–21, 1969.

86. Quoted in Phineas Israeli, "The God Game," *Berkeley Barb,* Feb. 14–21, 1969.

87. Quoted in John Wilcock, "Other Scenes," *Fifth Estate,* Nov. 27–Dec. 10, 1969.

88. "Sex Freedom League Aims Clarified," *Berkeley Barb,* Apr. 15, 1966.

89. Leonard Magruder, "A Middle Aged Beatnik Among the Hippies," *Notes from the Underground,* Jan. 17–31, 1968.

90. Braden, *Age of Aquarius,* 17, 258.

91. Paul Krassner (interview), "LSD, Revolution and God," *San Francisco Oracle* 1.6 (1967).

92. Thane Gower Ritalin, "The Hippies and the Hypocrites," *Seed,* Aug. 11–25, 1967.

93. Ralph J. Gleason, "The Final Paroxysm of Fear," *Rolling Stone,* Apr. 6, 1968.

94. Rubin, "Rubin Raps."

95. Abbie Hoffman, quoted in Melville, *Communes in the Counter Culture,* 109.

96. See Braden, *Age of Aquarius,* 159.

97. Roszak, *Making of a Counter Culture,* 205–38.

98. Ibid., 51.

99. Goodman, "New Reformation," 33.

Chapter 6
Legacy

1. Henry Steele Commager, *The American Mind* (New Haven, CT: Yale Univ. Press, 1950), 22.

2. For a history of the "back-to-nature" tradition in America prior to hippie times, see Peter J. Schmitt, *Back to Nature: The Arcadian Myth in Urban America* (New York: Oxford Univ. Press, 1969).

3. See Hal Sears, *The Sex Radicals: Free Love in High Victorian America* (Lawrence: Regents Press of Kansas, 1977); Joanne Ellen Passet, *The Sex Radicals and the Quest for Women's Equality* (Urbana: Univ. of Illinois Press, 2003).

4. National Commission on Marihuana and Drug Abuse, *Marihuana: A Signal of Misunderstanding,* 7.

5. John A. O'Donnell et al., *Young Men and Drugs—A Nationwide Survey* (Rockville, MD: National Institute on Drug Abuse, 1976).

6. Tom Siegfried, "Addiction," *Kansas City Star,* June 20, 1989, T2; originally published in the Dallas *Morning News.*

7. See http://www.cdc.gov/HealthyYouth/alcoholdrug/index.htm (accessed Aug. 12, 2010).

8. See, for example, R. R. Griffiths, W. A. Richards, M. W. Johnson, U. D. McCann, and R. Jesse, "Mystical-type Experiences Occasioned by Psilocybin Mediate the Attribution of Personal Meaning and Spiritual Significance 14 Months Later," *Journal of Psychopharmacology* 22.6 (Aug. 2008): 621–32.

9. George H. Gallup, *The Gallup Poll* (New York: Random House, 1972), vol. 3: 2216.

10. "The New Morality," *Time,* Nov. 21, 1977, 111–16.

11. See Gallup poll results at http://www.gallup.com/poll/27757/Americans-Rate-Morality-Social-Issues.aspx (accessed Aug. 11, 2010).

12. See Gallup poll results at http://www.gallup.com/poll/128291/americans-opposition-gay-marriage-eases-slightly.aspx (accessed Aug. 11, 2010).

13. Ginsberg, "Playboy Interview," 240.

14. John Gabree, "The System: Venceremos?" *Fusion,* Nov. 12, 1971, 34.

15. Wolfe, *Electric Kool-Aid Acid Test,* 361.

16. Mungo, *Famous Long Ago,* 117–18.

17. Craig Dremann, "Hippie Ethnobotany," *Whole Earth Review* 64 (Fall 1989): 25.

18. Kimbrell, "Coming Era of Activism," 66–68.

19. See, for example, Carol Clurman, "More than Just a Paycheck," *USA Weekend,* Jan. 19–21, 1990, 4–5. Many details of the social policies and economic and environmental activism of Ben and Jerry's are spelled out on the company's website at http://www.benjerry.com (accessed Aug. 12, 2010).

20. Roderick Frazier Nash, *The Rights of Nature: A History of Environmental Ethics* (Madison: Univ. of Wisconsin Press, 1989), 166.

21. Rachel Carson, *Silent Spring* (Boston: Houghton Mifflin, 1962).

22. Mark Satin, "Drugs Are Not the Enemy," *New Options* 62 (Nov. 27, 1989): 1.

23. Dorothy P. Rice, "Economic Costs of Substance Abuse, 1995," *Proceedings of the Association of American Physicians* 111.2 (Mar.–Apr. 1999): 119–25.

24. Ali H. Mokdad, James S. Marks, Donna F. Stroup, and Julie L. Gerberding, "Actual Causes of Death in the United States, 2000," *Journal of the American Medical Association* 291.10 (Mar. 10, 2004): 1238–45.

25. Statistics from the National Cancer Institute, available at http://www.cancer. gov/cancertopics/tobacco/statisticssnapshot (accessed Aug. 12, 2010).

26. Jerry Falwell, as quoted by William J. Petersen and Stephen Board, "Where Is Jerry Falwell Going?" *Eternity* 31.7 (July–Aug. 1980): 18–19. Quoted in *The Fundamentalist Phenomenon,* ed. Jerry Falwell (Garden City, NY: Doubleday, 1981), 144.

27. Another flip-flop of positions has occurred in the matter of a coming (or already present) age of abundance, the arrival of the end of scarcity. Some hippies once believed that modern society was productive enough to provide abundance to all (see chapter 6), but today the overwhelming majority of them see the world as moving headlong into severe scarcity—indeed, into the collapse of industrial civilization. Conservatives, once known for their dedication to the preservation of scarce resources, now often see such abundance at hand, apparently believing that resources such as oil, food, and water can support an expanding population indefinitely.

28. Ingrid Komar, *Living the Dream: A Documentary Study of Twin Oaks* (Norwood, PA: Norwood Editions, 1983).

29. Personal communication.

30. The book that resulted from those interviews was Timothy Miller, *The 60s Communes* (Syracuse: Syracuse Univ. Press, 1999). The largest numbers of interviews were conducted by Professor Deborah Altus of Washburn University.

Bibliography

Underground Newspapers

Nearly all of these papers are included in the Bell and Howell Underground Newspaper Collection, which consists of sixty-eight rolls of microfilm and covers hundreds of titles beyond those cited in this book. *Rolling Stone* is not included in Bell and Howell; I used a complete run in the hands of a private collector. In a very few cases I owned personal file copies of specific issues of papers that had been omitted from Bell and Howell.

American Avatar (New York and Boston)

American Dream (Tempe)

Argus (Ann Arbor)

Avatar (Boston)

Baltimore Free Press

Berkeley Barb

Berkeley Tribe

Big Us (Cleveland)

Buffalo Chip (Omaha)

Connections (Madison)

Daily Planet (Miami)

Dallas Notes

Deserted Times (San Francisco)

Distant Drummer (Philadelphia)

Dock of the Bay (San Francisco)

East Village Other (New York)

Fifth Estate (Detroit)

First Issue (Ithaca)

Florida Free Press (Jacksonville)

Good Times (San Francisco)

Great Speckled Bird (Atlanta)

Haight-Ashbury Tribune (San Francisco)

Hair (Minneapolis)

Hartford's Other Voice

Helix (Seattle)

Heterodoxical Voice (Newark, DE)

Hips Voice (Santa Fe)

Jabberwock (New York)

Kaleidoscope (Madison)

Kudzu (Jackson, MS)

Los Angeles Free Press

Los Angeles Underground

Middle Earth (Iowa City)

Mile High Underground (Denver)

New Hard Times (St. Louis)

Nola Express (New Orleans)

North Carolina Anvil (Durham)

Northwest Passage (Seattle)

Old Mole (Cambridge)

Open Process (San Francisco)

Oracle of Southern California (Los Angeles)

Other Scenes (New York)

Polar Star (Fairbanks)

Rag (Austin)

Raisin Bread (Minneapolis)

Rat (New York)

Resurrection (Tucson)

Rolling Stone (San Francisco)

San Diego Free Press

San Francisco Oracle

Seed (Chicago)

Seventy-Nine Cent Spread (Carmel, CA)

Space City News (Houston)

Speak Easy (Attleboro, MA)

Spectator (Bloomington)

Spokane Natural

Underground Review

Vortex (Lawrence and Kansas City)

Walrus (Champaign, IL)

Washington Free Press

Willamette Bridge (Portland, OR)

Xanadu (St. Louis)

Yarrow Stalks (Philadelphia)

Zig Zag (Montague, MA)

Direct predecessor and successor papers were also used; for example, the *San Francisco Express-Times*, the direct forerunner of *Good Times*, was used in the study on the same basis as its successor paper.

Books and Articles

This bibliography does not include citations of articles from the underground papers used in the study or others from the Bell and Howell Collection (see list above). Those articles are fully cited in the notes.

Abramson, H. A., ed. *The Use of LSD in Psychotherapy and Alcoholism.* Indianapolis: Bobbs-Merrill, 1967.

Ald, Roy. *The Youth Communes.* New York: Tower, 1970.

Allegro, John. *The Sacred Mushroom and the Cross.* London: Hodder and Stoughton, 1970.

Banner, Lois W. *Women in Modern America: A Brief History.* 2d ed. San Diego: Harcourt Brace Jovanovich, 1984.

Berke, Joseph, ed. *Counter Culture.* London: Peter Owen, 1969.

Braden, William. *The Age of Aquarius.* Cleveland: Quadrangle, 1970.

Carey, James T. "The Ideology in Popular Lyrics: A Content Analysis." In *Society's Shadow,* ed. Kenneth Westhues, 92–110. Toronto: McGraw-Hill Ryerson, 1972.

Carson, Rachel. *Silent Spring.* Boston: Houghton Mifflin, 1962.

Carter, David, ed. *Allen Ginsberg: Spontaneous Mind: Selected Interviews 1958–1996.* New York: Perennial/HarperCollins, 2001.

Claiborne, Robert. "Buying Time and Safety: Let's Legalize Heroin." *Village Voice,* Dec. 16, 1971.

Clark, Walter Houston. *Chemical Ecstasy.* New York: Sheed and Ward, 1969.

Clurman, Carol. "More than Just a Paycheck." *USA Weekend,* Jan. 19–21, 1990, 4–5.

Commager, Henry Steele. *The American Mind.* New Haven: Yale Univ. Press, 1950.

Cox, Harvey. "God and the Hippies." *Playboy* 15.1 (Jan. 1968): 93+.

Dedeaux, P. N. "Sade Lib." *Village Voice,* May 13, 1971.

DeMott, Benjamin. "Rock as Salvation." In *Pop Culture in America,* ed. David Manning White, 191–204. Originally published in the *New York Times Magazine,* Aug. 25, 1968.

Dremann, Craig. "Hippie Ethnobotany." *Whole Earth Review,* no. 64 (Fall 1989): 25.

Eisen, Jonathan, ed. *Altamont: Death of Innocence in the Woodstock Nation.* New York: Avon, 1970.

Eliade, Mircea. *Mephistopheles and the Androgyne.* New York: Sheed and Ward, 1965.

Falwell, Jerry, ed. *The Fundamentalist Phenomenon.* Garden City, NY: Doubleday, 1981.

Ferrandino, Joseph. "Rock Culture and the Development of Social Consciousness." In *Power to the People: New Left Writings,* ed. William Slate. New York: Tower, 1970, 173–95.

Gabree, John. "The System: Venceremos?" *Fusion* (Nov. 12, 1971): 32–34.

[Gaskin, Stephen.] *Hey Beatnik! This Is the Farm Book!* Summertown, TN: Book Publishing Co., 1974.

Ginsberg, Allen. "The Great Marijuana Hoax." *Atlantic Monthly* 218.5 (Nov. 1966): 104ff.

———. "Playboy Interview." *Playboy* 16.4 (Apr. 1969): 81+.

Gleason, Ralph J. "Bob Dylan and the Children's Crusade." *Conversations with the New Reality.* Ed. *Ramparts* editors. San Francisco: Canfield Press, 1971.

Goodman, Paul. *New Reformation.* New York: Random House, 1970.

———. "The New Reformation." *New York Times Magazine,* Sept. 14, 1969, 32+.

Gravy, Wavy. *Something Good for a Change: Random Notes on Peace Thru Living.* New York: St. Martin's, 1992.

Griffiths, R. R., W. A. Richards, M. W. Johnson, U. D. McCann, and R. Jesse. "Mystical-type Experiences Occasioned by Psilocybin Mediate the Attribution of Personal Meaning and Spiritual Significance 14 Months Later." *Journal of Psychopharmacology* 22.6 (Aug. 2008): 621–32.

Gruen, John. *The New Bohemia.* New York: Grosset and Dunlap, 1966.

Hoffman, Abbie. *Steal This Book.* New York: Grove, 1971.

Houriet, Robert. *Getting Back Together.* New York: Coward, McCann and Geohegan, 1971.

Huizinga, Johan. *Homo Ludens: A Study of the Play Element in Culture.* London: Routledge and Kegan Paul, 1949.

Jerome, Judson. *Families of Eden: Communes and the New Anarchism.* New York: Seabury, 1974.

Kanter, Rosabeth Moss. *Commitment and Community: Communes and Utopias in Sociological Perspective.* Cambridge: Harvard Univ. Press, 1972.

Keniston, Kenneth. *Young Radicals: Notes on Committed Youth.* New York: Harcourt, Brace and World, 1968.

Kimbrell, Andrew. "The Coming Era of Activism: New Left Meets New Age." *Utne Reader,* Mar.–Apr. 1988, 63–69.

Kleps, Art. *The Boo-Hoo Bible.* San Cristobal, NM: Toad Press, 1971.

Kolb, Terry. "Masochist's Lib." *Village Voice,* May 13, 1971.

Komar, Ingrid. *Living the Dream: A Documentary Study of Twin Oaks.* Norwood, PA: Norwood Editions, 1983.

Krassner, Paul, and Ken Kesey. "An Impolite Interview with Ken Kesey." *Realist,* May–June 1971, 1, 46–53. Reprinted in *The Best of the Realist,* ed. Paul Krassner (Philadelphia: Running Press, 1984), 213–22.

Kupferberg, Tuli. "The Coming Catastrophic Age of Leisure." In *Counter Culture,* ed. Joseph Berke, 74–87. London: Peter Owen, 1969.

Kurland, Albert A. "The Therapeutic Potential of LSD in Medicine." In *LSD, Man and Society,* ed. Richard C. DeBold and Russell C. Leaf, 20–35. Middletown, CT: Wesleyan Univ. Press, 1967.

Leamer, Laurence. *The Paper Revolutionaries: The Rise of the Underground Press.* New York: Simon and Schuster, 1972.

Leary, Timothy. *High Priest.* New York: World, 1968.

———. Introduction. In *LSD: The Consciousness-Expanding Drug,* ed. David Solomon, 11–28. New York: G. P. Putnam's Sons, 1964.

———. "Playboy Interview." *Playboy* 13.9 (Sept. 1966): 93+.

———. "The Politics, Ethics, and Meaning of Marijuana." In *The Marihuana Papers,* ed. David Solomon, 121–40. New York: New American Library, 1966.

———. *The Politics of Ecstasy.* New York: G. P. Putnam's Sons, 1968.

———. "The Religious Experience: Its Production and Interpretation." *Journal of Psychedelic Drugs* 1.2 (Winter 1967). Reprinted in *The Psychedelic Reader,* ed. Gunther M. Weil, Ralph Metzner, and Timothy Leary, 191–213. Secaucus, NJ: Citadel Press, 1965.

Leary, Timothy, Ralph Metzner, and Richard Alpert. *The Psychedelic Experience.* New Hyde Park, NY: University Books, 1964.

Lee, Martin A., and Bruce Schlain. *Acid Dreams: The CIA, LSD and the Sixties Rebellion.* New York: Grove Press, 1985.

Mailer, Norman. *The Armies of the Night.* New York: New American Library, 1968.

———. "The White Negro." In *Voices of Dissent,* 197–214. New York: Grove, 1958.

"Marijuana Laws." *Gallup Report* no. 241 (Oct. 1985): 28–30.

Masters, R. E. L., and Jean Houston. *The Varieties of Psychedelic Experience.* New York: Dell, 1966.

Matthews, Mark. *Droppers: America's First Hippie Commune, Drop City.* Norman: Univ. of Oklahoma Press, 2010.

Melville, Keith. *Communes in the Counter Culture.* New York: William Morrow, 1972.

Miller, Timothy. "Drug Bust in Kansas." *Christian Century* 88.11 (Mar. 17, 1971): 332–33.

———. *The 60s Communes.* Syracuse: Syracuse Univ. Press, 1999.

Mokdad, Ali H., James S. Marks, Donna F. Stroup, and Julie L. Gerberding. "Actual Causes of Death in the United States, 2000." *Journal of the American Medical Association* 291.10 (Mar. 10, 2004): 1238–45.

Moody, Howard. "Heroin: The Law Is Worse than the Drug." *Village Voice,* Sept. 14, 1972.

Moore, LeRoy Jr. "From Profane to Sacred America: Religion and the Cultural Revolution in the United States." *Journal of the American Academy of Religion* 39.3 (Sept. 1971): 321–38.

Mungo, Raymond. *Famous Long Ago: My Life and Hard Times with Liberation News Service.* Boston: Beacon, 1970.

———. *Total Loss Farm: A Year in the Life.* New York: Dutton, 1970.

Murphy, Karen, and Ronald Gross. "All You Need Is Love. Love Is All You Need." In *Pop Culture in America,* ed. David Manning White, 205–21. Chicago: Quadrangle, 1970. Originally published in the *New York Times Magazine,* Apr. 13, 1969.

Nash, Roderick Frazier. *The Rights of Nature: A History of Environmental Ethics.* Madison: Univ. of Wisconsin Press, 1989.

National Commission on Marihuana and Drug Abuse. *Marihuana: A Signal of Misunderstanding.* Official Report of the National Commission on Marihuana and Drug Abuse. New York: New American Library, 1972.

Nederland, Harold. "Asexuals Have Problems Too." *Village Voice,* Feb. 25, 1971.

Neville, Richard. *Play Power.* London: Jonathan Cape, 1970.

"The New Morality." *Time,* Nov. 21, 1977, 111.

O'Donnell, John A., et al. *Young Men and Drugs—A Nationwide Survey.* Rockville, MD: National Institute on Drug Abuse, 1976.

"Opinion Roundup: Societal Indicators." *Public Opinion* 10.4 (Nov.–Dec. 1987): 21–40.

Orth, Maureen. "Giving $14,905 Away: A Hip Soap Opera." *Village Voice,* Oct. 21, 1971.

Pahnke, Walter N. "Drugs and Mysticism: An Analysis of the Relationship between Psychedelic Drugs and the Mystical Consciousness." PhD diss., Harvard Univ., 1963.

Passet, Joanne Ellen. *The Sex Radicals and the Quest for Women's Equality.* Urbana: Univ. of Illinois Press, 2003.

Peck, Abe. *Uncovering the Sixties: The Life and Times of the Underground Press.* New York: Pantheon, 1985.

Perry, Helen Swick. *The Human Be-In.* New York: Basic Books, 1970.

Peterson, William J., and Stephen Board. "Where Is Jerry Falwell Going?" *Eternity* 31.7 (July–Aug. 1980): 18–19. Quoted in *The Fundamentalist Phenomenon,* ed. Jerry Falwell (Garden City, NY: Doubleday, 1981).

"Premarital Sex." *Gallup Report* no. 263 (Aug. 1987): 20–22.

Reich, Charles. *The Greening of America.* New York: Random House, 1970.

Rice, Dorothy P. "Economic Costs of Substance Abuse, 1995." *Proceedings of the Association of American Physicians* 111.2 (Mar.–Apr. 1999): 119–25.

Romm, Ethel Grodzins. *The Open Conspiracy.* Harrisburg, PA: Stackpole Books, 1970.

Roszak, Theodore. *The Making of a Counter Culture.* Garden City, NY: Doubleday, 1969.

Rubin, Jerry. *Do It!* New York: Simon and Schuster, 1970.

———. *We Are Everywhere.* New York: Harper and Row, 1971.

Sanders, Ed. *The Family.* New York: Dutton, 1970.

Satin, Mark. "Drugs Are Not the Enemy." *New Options* no. 62 (Nov. 27, 1989): 1.

Schmitt, Peter J. *Back to Nature: The Arcadian Myth in Urban America.* New York: Oxford Univ. Press, 1969.

Schwartz, Ed. "Why Communes Fail." *Fusion* (Nov. 12, 1971): 20–25.

Sears, Hal. *The Sex Radicals: Free Love in High Victorian America.* Lawrence: Regents Press of Kansas, 1977.

Shepherd, William C. "Counter Cultural Religiosity: A Reply to Bellah, Baum, and Lidz." *Sociological Inquiry* 42.2 (1972): 168–72.

———. "Religion and the Counter Culture—A New Religiosity." *Sociological Inquiry* 42.1 (1972): 3–9.

Siegel, Jules. "West of Eden." *Playboy* 17.11 (Nov. 1970): 174+.

Simmons, J. L., and Barry Winograd. *It's Happening.* Santa Barbara, CA: Marc-Laird Publications, 1966.

Slater, Philip N. *The Pursuit of Loneliness: American Culture at the Breaking Point.* Boston: Beacon, 1970.

Smith, Howard. "Scenes." *Village Voice,* Apr. 22, 1971.

Stach, Alex G. "Hippie Communes U.S.A.: Five Case Studies, 1970." PhD diss., Univ. of Minnesota, 1971.

Stafford, Peter, ed. *Psychedelic Baby Reaches Puberty.* New York: Praeger, 1971.

Stokes, Geoffrey. "The Sixties." In *Rock of Ages: The Rolling Stone History of Rock and Roll,* ed. Ed Ward, Geoffrey Stokes, and Ken Tucker, 247–463. New York: Summit Books/Simon and Schuster, 1986.

Tipton, Steven M. *Getting Saved from the Sixties: Moral Meaning in Conversion and Cultural Change.* Berkeley: Univ. of California Press, 1982.

Tosches, Nick. "Getting Out the Vote." *Fusion* (Nov. 26, 1971): 28–31.

Traugot, Michael . *A Short History of the Farm.* Summertown, TN: Author, 1994.

Truscott, Lucian K. "Chop, Chop: Age of Psychedelic Fascism." *Village Voice,* Oct. 14, 1971.

Wasson, R. Gordon. *Soma: Divine Mushroom of Immortality.* New York: Harcourt, Brace and World, 1969.

Watts, Alan. "Wealth Versus Money." *Playboy* 15.12 (Dec. 1968): 210+.

Weil, Andrew. *The Natural Mind.* Boston: Houghton Mifflin, 1972.

Westhues, Kenneth, ed. *Society's Shadow: Studies in the Sociology of Countercultures.* Toronto: McGraw-Hill Ryerson, 1972.

White, David Manning, ed. *Pop Culture in America.* Chicago: Quadrangle, 1970.

Wolf, Leonard, ed. *Voices from the Love Generation.* Boston: Little, Brown, 1968.

Wolfe, Tom. *The Electric Kool-Aid Acid Test.* New York: Farrar, Straus and Giroux, 1968.

Yablonsky, Lewis. *The Hippie Trip.* New York: Pegasus, 1968.

"Youth: The Hippies." *Time,* July 7, 1967, 18–22.

Index

Cleaver, Eldridge, xxi
clothing, 99, 111
Clurman, Carol, 146n19
cocaine, 2, 20, 117, 118
Commager, Henry Steele, 106
communes, xviii, xx, 6, 73–85, 108;
    dope and, 75–76, 84; estimates of
    numbers of, 74; individualism and
    collectivism, 83–85; as means, not
    ends, 76–77; and new family struc-
    tures, 75–79, 108; problems with,
    81–83; and rock festivals, 74–75;
    rural setting of, 76, 77–78; types of,
    79–80; women and, 81–82. *See also*
    specific communes
community, 49
Cox, Harvey, xxv
Crosby, David, 22
crack. *See* cocaine
Curb, Mike, 23

death of hip, xiii, 90
DeBold, Richard C., 131n101
Dedeaux, P. N., 133n12
Diggers, xiii, 89, 90
dirt, 98, 100–101
DMT, 2
dope and drugs, 1–23, 108–9, 117;
    and awareness of nature, 14; and
    communes, 76; and creativity, 18;
    distinction among, 1–3; ethical case
    for, 9–18; and fun, 1–17; harmless-
    ness of, 17; incidence of use, 3–5,
    110; and interpersonal relations, 15;
    legalization of, 6–7, 118; medical
    uses of, 18; opposition to, 19–23;
    and politics, 92; reasons for using,
    5–6; and religion, 7–9, 10–14; and
    rock music, 44, 49; and sex, 14–15,
    37; terminology, 1–2; unethical use
    of, 20–21
Dr. Hippocrates. *See* Schoenfeld, Eugene
Douglas, William O., 29

Doukhobors, 32
Dragonwagon, Crescent, 98
Dremann, Craig, 114
Drop City, 74
dropping out, 93–94
drugs. *See* dope and drugs
du Bois, W. E. B., xvi
Dylan, Bob, xvi, 42, 45, 46–47, 113–14

Earth Day, 116
Earth First!, 116
Earth People's Park, 78
Ecovillage Training Center, 121
Eisen, Jonathan, 45, 139n47
Eliade, Mircea, 99
Ellis, Albert, 26, 107, 133n5
environmental ethics, 92–93, 108, 116
Eric Burdon and War (rock band), 23
Estellachild, Vivian, 81

Faber, David, 19
Falwell, Jerry, 120
Farm (commune), 6, 36, 80, 121
Fellowship of the Clear Light, 9
feminism, hippie influence on, xxiv–xxv,
    26, 38, 116
Fersh, Don, 76, 80
Fletcher, Andrew, 45
Foster, Marilyn, 82
Foundation Church/Foundation Faith,
    132n126
Fritz, Leah, 26
Fugs (rock band), 46

Gabree, John, 112
Gallup poll, 146n11, 146n12
Garcia, Jerry, 113
Garrison, Daniel H., 134n23
Gaskin, Stephen, 6, 36, 80
Gay Liberation Front, 30, 33
generation gap, xviii–xix
Ginsberg, Allen, xiii, xvi, xvii, xix, xxix,
    45, 78, 96; and dope/drugs, 2, 6, 18,

19, 20, 21, 22; on the impact of the
counterculture, 111, 117
Gleason, Ralph J., xxi, xxvi, 45, 47, 91, 102
Gold, Steve, 23
Good Friday study, 12
Goodman, Paul, xx, xxi, xxix, 84
Gorkin, 76
Gottlieb, Lou, 78
Grateful Dead, 42, 113
Gravy, Wavy, 50, 78
Greeley, Horace, 82
Greenpeace, 116
Griffiths. R. R., 146n8
Grinnell College, 32
Gross, Ronald, 137n6
Gwin, Pam, 134n17

Haight-Ashbury, 90, 121
hair, 98–99, 111
Hare Krishnas, 39, 80
Harmonists, 73
Harrison, George, 92
hashish, 2
Hawaiian wood rose, 20
Hayden, Tom, 39
health food, 114
hedonism, 101–2, 109
Hefner, Hugh, 31
Hells Angels, 15, 50
heroin, 19, 20, 39, 44, 117, 118
Hitler, Adolf, xviii
Hodenfield, Jan, 3
Hoffman, Abbie, xvii, 2, 45, 94, 96, 98,
102
Hog Farm (commune), 75, 78
Holly, Buddy, xvi
homosexuality, 26, 28, 110–11, 117
Houriet, Robert, 77
Houston, Jean, 12
Huizinga, Johan, 95
Hutterites, 73
hypocrisy, 102

Iverson, Stan, xx

Jarvis, Ron, 41, 42, 45, 96
Jerome, Judson, 74
Jesse, R., 146n8
Jesus freaks, 80
Johnson, M. W, 146n8
Johnston, Art, xvii
Joplin, Janis, 105

Kanter, Rosabeth Moss, 74
Keniston, Kenneth, 95
Kesey, Ken, 11, 20, 35, 36
Kimbrell, Andrew, xxiii, 114
Kleps, Art, 6, 8
Kolb, Terry, 133n12
Kopkind, Andrew, xix, 50
Krassner, Paul, xvi, 11, 102
Krippner, Stanley, 76, 80
Kunkin, Art, 21
Kupferberg, Tuli, 75, 87, 96
Kurland, Albert A., 131n101

Lama Foundation, 80
Landau, Jon, 48
Laurence, Leo, 135n53
Leaf, Russell C., 131n101
League for Spiritual Discovery, 8
Leamer, Lawrence, xxi
Leary, Timothy, xvii, xxi, xxix, 50, 93,
128n52; on psychedelics, 1, 2, 3, 6,
8, 11, 14, 16, 19, 21, 37; on sex, 34,
37; on communes, 74, 77, 79, 84; on
hedonism, 101
Lebel, Jean-Jacques, xvii
Leder, Kit, 81
Lennon, John, xvi, 47–48
Levine, Steve, 137n10
Liberation News Service, 18
Lipton, Lawrence, xviii, 94
Little Richard, xvi
Love Conspiracy Commune, 90
Love Ethic, 88–90

Somerville, Don H., 28
speed. *See* amphetamines
Stafford, P. G., xx, 13, 44
Starr, Ringo, 44
Stokes, Geoffrey, 42, 139n47
Stonewall police raid, 29
STP, 2
Student National Coordinating Committee, xx
Students for a Democratic Society (SDS), xx, 45
Summer of Love, xiii, xv, xxv
"Super-Straight, David," xxii

Taub, Edward, 46
theft, ethics of, 97–98
Thorne, Richard, 33
Tipton, Steven, xv
Toad Hall (commune), 82
Tolstoy Farm (commune), 74
Truscott, Lucian, 21
truth and hypocrisy, 102
Twin Oaks (commune), 121

underground press, xxvii–xxix
Underground Press Collection, 125n57
University Microfilms, 125n57

Vietnam war, xxi, xxii, 89, 91, 111

Wasson, R. Gordon, 129n74
Watts, Alan, 94
Weathermen, 45
Weil, Andrew, 16, 17
Westhues, Kenneth, 97
Wheelock, Mick, xxi
White, David Manning, 137n6
Whole Earth Catalog, 94
Williams, Andy, 42
Winograd, Barry, xiv, 46
WITCH (Women's International Terrorist Conspiracy from Hell), 38
Wittman, Carl, 134n21
Wolf, Leonard and Deborah, 137n10
Wolfe, Tom, 112
Women's Liberation Health Collective, 35
women's liberation movement, 38
Woodstock festival, xix, xxii, 2, 45, 49–51, 75, 84, 94; and community, 78; and dope/drugs, 3, 4; nudity at, 30
work and play, 95–97, 109

Yablonsky, Lewis, 4, 93
Yasgur, Max, 50

Zablocki, Benjamin, 74
Zen Buddhists, 15